Paris Travel Guide

The Essential Pocket Guide to the City of Light. Discover All You Need to Know About Paris and Plan Your Next Trip

Benoit Lemaigre

are for clarifying purposes only and are the owned by the owners themselves, not affiliated with this document.

TABLE OF CONTENTS

PARIS

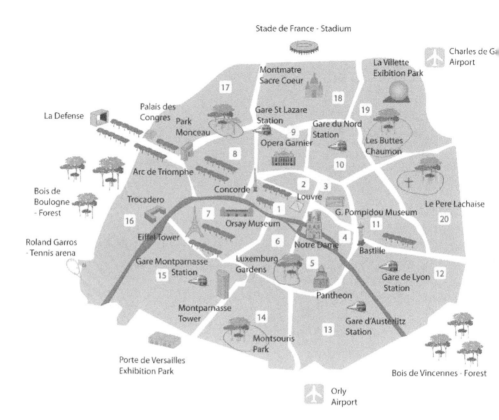

INTRODUCTION

Bonjour, friends! Before we dive into exploring the enchanting city of Paris, allow me to introduce myself. I'm Benoit Lemaigre, and it's my pleasure to guide you through the wonders of Paris, my beloved city. Born and raised in the heart of France, I've spent countless hours wandering its streets, discovering its secrets, and falling in love with its unique charm. Over the years, I've had the privilege of sharing my insights with friends and travelers from around the world, helping them experience the true essence of Paris beyond the typical tourist trails.

This inspired me to create this pocket guide, meticulously organized by arrondissement, so I can share my insider knowledge of Paris's hidden gems—the places and experiences that embody the true Parisian culture and spirit. As we explore each arrondissement, I'll recommend sights not to miss, quintessential foods to sample, and activities that will allow you to mingle with locals and make lifelong memories. Because, after all, it is the people who make Paris what it is.

Paris's 20 arrondissements are like individual villages, each with its own distinct personality and charm. From the historic grandeur of the 1st arrondissement, home to the Louvre and Tuileries Garden, to the artistic soul of Montmartre in the 18th, each area offers unique experiences and adventures. Whether you seek the bohemian atmosphere of the Latin Quarter, the luxury of the Champs-Élysées, or the multicultural vibrancy of Belleville, this guide will help you uncover the best of each neighborhood.

Focus on Authentic Experiences

One of the main goals of this guide is to help you experience Paris as the locals do. While famous landmarks like the Eiffel Tower and Notre-Dame are undoubtedly worth visiting, the true magic of Paris lies in its everyday moments and hidden corners. I'll share my favorite spots for enjoying a leisurely coffee, the best streets for a romantic evening stroll, and the most atmospheric markets for picking up fresh produce and artisanal goods.

For example, instead of just visiting the Musée d'Orsay, why not also explore the nearby Rue de Bac, with its charming shops and cafes? Or after marveling at the grandeur of the Arc de Triomphe, take a detour to the quieter, leafy streets of the 16th arrondissement, where you can find beautiful Art Nouveau architecture and serene parks.

Culinary Delights

No exploration of Paris would be complete without indulging in its world-renowned cuisine. Each arrondissement has its own culinary specialties and beloved eateries. I'll guide you to the best patisseries for a morning croissant, the coziest bistros for a hearty French meal, and the finest wine bars for an evening aperitif. We'll uncover the secrets of the city's best cheese shops, bakeries, and chocolate boutiques, ensuring that every meal is a memorable one.

In the 11th arrondissement, for instance, you can discover some of the trendiest restaurants and bars, where innovative chefs are redefining French cuisine. Meanwhile, the 12th offers the bustling Marché d'Aligre, a local market where you can taste fresh oysters and sip a glass of white wine with the locals.

Cultural Immersion

Paris is a city of art and culture, where history and modernity coexist in a beautiful tapestry. Beyond the famous museums and galleries, I'll introduce you to lesser-known cultural spots that offer a more intimate experience. From independent art galleries in the Marais to small theaters in the 9th arrondissement, there are countless ways to immerse yourself in the city's vibrant cultural scene.

Attend a classical music concert in a historic church, explore a quirky contemporary art exhibition, or join a local book club discussion at a charming bookstore. These experiences will give you a deeper appreciation of Paris's artistic heritage and contemporary creativity.

Connecting with Locals

One of the most rewarding aspects of travel is forming connections with people. In Paris, you'll find that locals are often eager to share their love for their city. I'll offer tips on how to engage with

Parisians, whether it's by striking up a conversation at a café, joining a neighborhood event, or participating in a local workshop.

For instance, you might join a cooking class in the 5th arrondissement to learn how to make classic French dishes, or participate in a wine tasting in the 20th to discover the nuances of French viticulture. These interactions will enrich your travel experience and provide lasting memories.

Practical Tips

This guide also includes practical information to help you navigate Paris with ease. From transportation tips to advice on finding the best accommodations, I'll provide all the details you need to make your trip smooth and enjoyable. Learn how to use the metro like a local, find the best times to visit popular attractions, and discover the most charming neighborhoods to stay in.

For example, I'll explain the intricacies of Paris's public transportation system, including the metro, buses, and Vélib' bike-sharing program, so you can move around the city efficiently. I'll also share tips on how to avoid long lines at major attractions and recommend quieter times to visit popular sites.

Embrace the Unexpected

Paris is a city that rewards the curious and the adventurous. While it's important to plan your itinerary,

it's equally important to leave room for spontaneity. Some of the most memorable travel experiences come from unexpected discoveries and chance encounters. Allow yourself to get lost in the city's labyrinthine streets, follow your instincts, and embrace the surprises that Paris has in store.

For instance, while exploring the winding streets of the Marais, you might stumble upon a hidden courtyard filled with blooming flowers, or find a charming antique shop with unique treasures. In the Latin Quarter, a leisurely stroll could lead you to a quiet, centuries-old bookshop where you can lose yourself in the pages of a classic novel.

Seasonal Highlights

Paris is a city for all seasons, each offering its own unique charm and experiences. This guide will highlight what makes each time of year special, from springtime blossoms and summer festivals to autumn's golden colors and winter's cozy ambiance.

In spring, the city comes alive with blooming flowers and outdoor events. Take a walk through the Jardin des Plantes or the Luxembourg Gardens to see the vibrant displays of tulips and cherry blossoms. Summer brings long days and warm evenings, perfect for picnics along the Seine or outdoor concerts in the parks. Autumn is a time for harvest festivals and enjoying the crisp air in the city's many green spaces. Winter transforms Paris into a magical wonderland, with festive lights, Christmas markets, and ice skating rinks.

Day Trips and Excursions

While Paris itself offers endless attractions, there are also many wonderful destinations just a short train ride away. This guide includes recommendations for day trips and excursions that will allow you to explore the beauty and diversity of the surrounding regions.

Consider a visit to the opulent Palace of Versailles, where you can wander through the grand halls and stunning gardens. Or take a trip to the charming town of Giverny, home to Monet's house and gardens, which inspired some of his most famous works. The historic city of Rouen, with its medieval architecture and vibrant cultural scene, is another great option for a day trip.

For those interested in wine, a visit to the picturesque vineyards of Champagne or the Loire Valley offers a delightful escape from the city. Explore the scenic countryside, tour historic châteaux, and taste world-class wines.

Customizing Your Experience

Every traveler is unique, and this guide is designed to help you create a personalized Parisian adventure based on your interests and passions. Whether you're an art lover, a history buff, a foodie, or an outdoor enthusiast, you'll find tailored recommendations to suit your preferences.

For art enthusiasts, I'll highlight must-see museums and galleries, as well as off-the-beaten-path art spaces. History buffs can explore the many layers of Paris's past, from Roman ruins to revolutionary landmarks. Foodies will discover the best places to indulge in everything from street food to haute cuisine. And for those who love the outdoors, I'll recommend the city's best parks, gardens, and scenic walking routes.

Final Thoughts

Paris is more than just a destination; it's an experience that stays with you long after you've returned home. Its beauty, elegance, and spirit leave an indelible mark on all who visit. This guide is your companion in uncovering the true essence of Paris, helping you to see beyond the tourist façade and connect with the city's heart and soul.

As you embark on your journey, remember to take your time, savor each moment, and open yourself to the magic of Paris. Whether you're visiting for a weekend or a month, let your curiosity lead you, and you'll discover a Paris that is uniquely yours.

How to Use This Guide

Think of this guide as your personal notebook, filled with insights and recommendations to enhance your Parisian adventure. When you come across something that excites you, mark it. If the description of a dish makes your mouth water, highlight it. Use this guide to plan your stay in Paris, ensuring you don't miss anything that sparks your imagination.

Sorry if there are any errors. While English-speaking experts have reviewed this book, there may still be some oversights. I hope your reading experience is enjoyable and that this guide serves as a valuable resource for your journey.

Now, let's begin our exploration of this enchanting city. Paris awaits, with its timeless beauty, captivating charm, and endless possibilities. Bon voyage!

Overview of the Arrondissements (Quartiers) of Paris

1st Arrondissement (Louvre)

Key Attractions: Louvre Museum, Palais Royal, Tuileries Garden

Character: Historic heart of Paris with world-renowned museums and elegant gardens.

2nd Arrondissement (Bourse)

Key Attractions: Palais Brongniart (former stock exchange), Rue Montorgueil, Passage des Panoramas

Character: Financial district with lively markets and historic shopping arcades.

3rd Arrondissement (Temple)

Key Attractions: Musée Picasso, Musée des Arts et Métiers, Le Marais (northern part)

Character: Trendy area with rich history, boutique shopping, and vibrant nightlife.

4th Arrondissement (Hôtel-de-Ville)

Key Attractions: Notre-Dame Cathedral, Hôtel de Ville, Le Marais (southern part)

Character: Historic and cultural hub, including the Jewish Quarter and LGBTQ+ friendly areas.

5th Arrondissement (Panthéon)

Key Attractions: Panthéon, Sorbonne University, Jardin des Plantes

Character: The Latin Quarter, known for its academic institutions, literary history, and lively student atmosphere.

6th Arrondissement (Luxembourg)

Key Attractions: Luxembourg Gardens, Saint-Germain-des-Prés, Odéon Theatre

Character: Chic and artistic, with high-end shops, cafes, and intellectual heritage.

7th Arrondissement (Palais-Bourbon)

Key Attractions: Eiffel Tower, Musée d'Orsay, Les Invalides

Character: Affluent and grand, featuring iconic landmarks and embassies.

8th Arrondissement (Élysée)

Key Attractions: Champs-Élysées, Arc de Triomphe, Place de la Concorde

Character: Luxury shopping and business district, home to many high-end hotels and restaurants.

9th Arrondissement (Opéra)

Key Attractions: Palais Garnier (Opera House), Galeries Lafayette, Musée Grévin

Character: Vibrant area with theaters, grand boulevards, and shopping.

10th Arrondissement (Entrepôt)

Key Attractions: Canal Saint-Martin, Gare du Nord, Gare de l'Est

Character: Bohemian and diverse, known for its canals and trendy bars.

11th Arrondissement (Popincourt)

Key Attractions: Place de la Bastille, Rue Oberkampf, Cirque d'Hiver

Character: Hip and lively, with a thriving nightlife and artistic community.

12th Arrondissement (Reuilly)

Key Attractions: Bois de Vincennes, Parc de Bercy, Opéra Bastille

Character: Green spaces and residential, with cultural venues and modern developments.

13th Arrondissement (Gobelins)

Key Attractions: Bibliothèque François Mitterrand, Butte-aux-Cailles, Chinatown

Character: Modern and multicultural, with notable contemporary architecture.

14th Arrondissement (Observatoire)

Key Attractions: Montparnasse Tower, Catacombs of Paris, Parc Montsouris

Character: Residential and artistic, with a mix of modern and historic elements.

15th Arrondissement (Vaugirard)

Key Attractions: Parc André Citroën, Beaugrenelle Shopping Center, Port de Javel

Character: Large, residential area offering a quieter, local Parisian lifestyle.

16th Arrondissement (Passy)

Key Attractions: Trocadéro, Bois de Boulogne, Musée Marmottan Monet

Character: Affluent and traditional, known for its elegant buildings and green spaces.

17th Arrondissement (Batignolles-Monceau)

Key Attractions: Parc Monceau, Palais des Congrès, Batignolles

Character: Diverse, with both upscale neighborhoods and more affordable areas.

18th Arrondissement (Butte-Montmartre)

Key Attractions: Montmartre, Sacré-Cœur Basilica, Moulin Rouge

Character: Bohemian and historic, with a strong artistic legacy and vibrant nightlife.

19th Arrondissement (Buttes-Chaumont)

Key Attractions: Parc des Buttes-Chaumont, Cité des Sciences et de l'Industrie, Parc de la Villette

Character: Diverse and dynamic, with large parks and cultural venues that attract families and young people.

20th Arrondissement (Ménilmontant)

Key Attractions: Père Lachaise Cemetery, Belleville, Parc de Belleville

Character: Bohemian and multicultural, known for its artistic community and vibrant street art scene.

1ST ARRONDISSEMENT (LOUVRE)

Main Interesting History Facts of the Arrondissement

The 1st Arrondissement of Paris is one of the city's most historic quarters, and it plays a pivotal role in the cultural and political history of France.

Early Beginnings

The area now known as the 1st Arrondissement has been inhabited since ancient times. The early settlers were the Parisii, a Gallic tribe who established a fishing village on the Île de la Cité around 250 BC. This settlement attracted the attention of the Romans, who conquered the Parisii and established the city of Lutetia on the left bank of the Seine.

Medieval Developments

In the medieval era, the 1st Arrondissement became the heart of the city. The construction of the Louvre began in the late 12th century under King Philippe Auguste, originally intended as a fortress to protect Paris from invaders. Over the centuries, it evolved from a defensive stronghold into a royal palace.

Renaissance Transformation

The Renaissance period saw significant changes in the 1st Arrondissement. King François I ordered the transformation of the Louvre into a magnificent palace, attracting artists and architects from across Europe. This era also saw the construction of the Tuileries Palace and gardens, commissioned by Queen Catherine de Medici in the 16th century.

Revolution and Modernization

The 1st Arrondissement played a central role during the French Revolution. The Tuileries Palace became a key site for revolutionary events, including the storming and the eventual imprisonment of King Louis XVI and Marie Antoinette. The palace was later burned down during the Paris Commune in 1871.

In the 19th century, Baron Haussmann's extensive renovations under Napoleon III modernized Paris, including the 1st

Arrondissement. The wide boulevards, elegant buildings, and public spaces we see today were largely shaped during this period.

Cultural Hub

Today, the 1st Arrondissement is a cultural hub, home to world-famous museums, historic landmarks, and beautiful gardens. It remains a testament to Paris's rich history and enduring legacy.

Things To Do You Can't Miss

The 1st Arrondissement offers a myriad of activities and sights that cater to all interests. Here are some must-do activities:

Visit the Louvre Museum

As the world's largest and most visited museum, the Louvre is an absolute must-see. Home to over 35,000 works of art, including the Mona Lisa and the Venus de Milo, it offers an unparalleled journey through art history.

Explore the Palais Royal

Originally built for Cardinal Richelieu, the Palais Royal is now a beautiful public space featuring elegant arcades, shops, and the stunning Palais Royal Garden. Don't miss the striking black and white striped columns of the Colonnes de Buren in the courtyard.

Stroll Through the Tuileries Garden

Created by Catherine de Medici in the 16th century, the Tuileries Garden is a perfect place for a leisurely stroll. Enjoy the manicured lawns, statues, fountains, and the stunning views of the Louvre and Place de la Concorde.

Discover Sainte-Chapelle

Located on the Île de la Cité, Sainte-Chapelle is renowned for its stunning stained glass windows, which depict biblical scenes in vivid colors. This Gothic chapel, built in the 13th century, is a masterpiece of medieval architecture.

Shop at Les Halles

Les Halles was once the bustling central market of Paris. Today, it's a modern shopping center known as Westfield Forum des Halles, featuring a wide range of shops, restaurants, and the impressive Canopy structure.

Famous Places

The 1st Arrondissement is home to some of the most iconic landmarks in Paris.

The Louvre Museum

As mentioned earlier, the Louvre Museum is an essential visit. Its iconic glass pyramid entrance, designed by I.M. Pei, is a modern complement to the historic palace.

Pont Neuf

Despite its name meaning "New Bridge," Pont Neuf is the oldest standing bridge across the Seine in Paris. It connects the Île de la Cité to both banks of the river and offers beautiful views of the city.

Place Vendôme

This elegant square is known for its grand architecture and luxury shops, including high-end jewelers and fashion houses. The central Vendôme Column commemorates Napoleon's victory at Austerlitz.

Conciergerie

Once a royal palace and later a prison during the French Revolution, the Conciergerie is now a historic site where you can learn about its fascinating past. It was here that Marie Antoinette was imprisoned before her execution.

Comédie-Française

Founded in 1680, the Comédie-Française is one of the few state theaters in France and the oldest still in use. It is dedicated to the preservation and performance of classic French theater, particularly the works of Molière. Attending a play here offers a glimpse into the rich tradition of French theatrical arts.

Pont des Arts

Known as the "Lover's Bridge," the Pont des Arts was once famous for the countless love locks attached to its railings. While the locks have been removed to preserve the bridge, it remains a popular spot for romantic strolls and offers stunning views of the Seine and the Parisian skyline.

Famous Restaurants

The 1st Arrondissement is a culinary paradise, offering a range of dining experiences from traditional French cuisine to international flavors. Here are some recommendations:

Angelina

This iconic tea house on Rue de Rivoli is famous for its rich hot chocolate and delectable pastries, particularly the Mont Blanc dessert. A visit to Angelina is a step back in time to the Belle Époque era.

Le Grand Véfour

Located in the Palais Royal, Le Grand Véfour is one of the oldest and most prestigious restaurants in Paris. Established in 1784, it has hosted famous figures such as Napoleon and Victor Hugo. The menu features refined French cuisine in an opulent setting.

Au Pied de Cochon

A historic brasserie near Les Halles, Au Pied de Cochon has been serving classic French dishes since 1947. Open 24/7, it's known for its hearty fare, including onion soup, escargots, and its namesake dish, pig's trotters.

What to Eat

The 1st Arrondissement is a melting pot of culinary delights, reflecting both traditional French cuisine and international influences. Here are some must-try dishes and culinary experiences:

Traditional French Dishes

- **Croissants and Pastries:** Start your day with a buttery croissant or pain au chocolat from a local bakery. The area is home to several renowned patisseries, including Pierre Hermé and Ladurée.
- **Onion Soup:** A classic Parisian dish, onion soup is a comforting choice, especially at traditional brasseries like Au Pied de Cochon.
- **Escargots:** For a true taste of France, try escargots (snails) prepared with garlic and parsley butter. L'Escargot Montorgueil is the perfect place to sample this delicacy.

- **Foie Gras:** This rich and luxurious dish is a staple of French cuisine. Enjoy it as an appetizer at upscale restaurants like Le Grand Véfour.

International Flavors

- **Japanese Cuisine:** The 1st Arrondissement is home to a vibrant Japanese culinary scene, particularly around Rue Sainte-Anne. Explore ramen shops, sushi bars, and izakayas for an authentic taste of Japan.
- **Chinese Cuisine:** For a unique fusion experience, Yam'Tcha offers a menu that blends French and Chinese flavors. Their innovative dishes and tea pairings provide a memorable dining experience.

Sweet Treats

- **Hot Chocolate:** Angelina's hot chocolate is legendary, known for its thick, velvety texture and rich flavor. Pair it with a pastry for a decadent treat.
- **Macarons:** Sample these delicate almond meringue cookies from renowned patisseries like Pierre Hermé and Ladurée. With a variety of flavors, macarons are a quintessential Parisian sweet.
- **Mont Blanc Dessert:** Angelina's signature Mont Blanc dessert, made with chestnut cream and meringue, is a must-try for those with a sweet tooth.

Summary

The 1st Arrondissement of Paris, also known as the Louvre, is a treasure trove of history, culture, and culinary delights. From its ancient beginnings as a Gallic settlement to its pivotal role in the French Revolution and its transformation into a modern cultural hub, this arrondissement encapsulates the essence of Paris.

Visitors can immerse themselves in the world-renowned art of the Louvre Museum, enjoy the tranquility of the Tuileries Garden, and explore historic landmarks like the Palais Royal and Sainte-Chapelle. The area's rich history is complemented by its vibrant present, with bustling shopping centers like Les Halles and iconic bridges like Pont Neuf.

Culinary enthusiasts will find a paradise of flavors, from traditional French dishes at historic brasseries to innovative fusion cuisine at Michelin-starred restaurants. Whether savoring a buttery croissant, indulging in a luxurious foie gras, or enjoying a cup of Angelina's famous hot chocolate, the 1st Arrondissement offers a dining experience to remember.

In essence, the 1st Arrondissement is a microcosm of Paris itself—a place where history meets modernity, art flourishes, and every meal is a celebration of the city's rich culinary heritage. Whether you're a history buff, an art lover, or a foodie, the 1st Arrondissement has something to offer everyone, making it an essential part of any visit to Paris.

2ND ARRONDISSEMENT (BOURSE)

Main Interesting History Facts of the Arrondissement

The 2nd Arrondissement, known as Bourse, is one of the smallest yet most historically significant areas in Paris. Its history is deeply intertwined with the commercial and financial life of the city.

Medieval Beginnings

The 2nd Arrondissement was initially part of the medieval city that expanded beyond its original boundaries on the Île de la Cité. During the Middle Ages, this area was known for its markets and trade. Rue Montorgueil, one of the oldest streets, was a major artery for goods entering the city from the north.

Financial Heart of Paris

The 19th century marked a significant transformation for the 2nd Arrondissement when it became the financial hub of Paris. The construction of the Bourse (Paris Stock Exchange), completed in 1826, cemented its status as the center of commerce. The Palais Brongniart, where the Bourse was housed, became a symbol of economic power.

Passageways and Galleries

The 2nd Arrondissement is famous for its covered passages, which date back to the early 19th century. These passages, such as Passage des Panoramas and Galerie Vivienne, were precursors to modern shopping malls, providing Parisians with elegant and weather-protected shopping venues. They housed boutiques, cafes, and entertainment venues, contributing to the arrondissement's vibrant commercial life.

Les Halles Market

Although Les Halles, the central market of Paris, was technically in the 1st Arrondissement, its influence extended into the 2nd. For centuries, Les Halles was the "stomach of Paris," supplying the city with fresh produce, meat, and fish. The market's bustling activity spilled over into the surrounding streets, including those in the 2nd Arrondissement.

Modern Developments

Today, the 2nd Arrondissement retains its commercial spirit but has also become a hub for technology and startups, particularly in the area known as "Silicon Sentier." The historical buildings now host a mix of traditional businesses and innovative tech companies, creating a dynamic blend of old and new.

Things To Do You Can't Miss

The 2nd Arrondissement offers a variety of activities that cater to different interests, from exploring historical sites to enjoying modern entertainment.

Explore the Covered Passages

Wandering through the covered passages is a quintessential Parisian experience. These elegant arcades are filled with charming boutiques, antique shops, and cozy cafes. Must-see passages include:

- **Passage des Panoramas:** The oldest covered passage in Paris, dating back to 1799. It is famous for its vintage shops and historic eateries.
- **Galerie Vivienne:** Known for its stunning mosaics and upscale boutiques. This passage offers a glimpse into the elegance of 19th-century Paris.
- **Passage Choiseul:** A lively passage with a mix of theaters, shops, and restaurants. It's a great spot for a leisurely stroll.

Visit the Bourse de Commerce

The Bourse de Commerce, once the home of the Paris Stock Exchange, has been transformed into a contemporary art museum under the auspices of the Pinault Collection. The building itself is an architectural marvel, blending historical elements with modern design. The art exhibitions here showcase works from some of the most influential contemporary artists.

Discover Rue Montorgueil

Rue Montorgueil is a bustling street known for its vibrant market atmosphere. Lined with bakeries, cheese shops, butchers, and cafes, it offers a taste of traditional Parisian life. This pedestrian-friendly street is perfect for a leisurely walk, shopping for gourmet products, and enjoying a meal at one of the many outdoor terraces.

Experience the Opéra Comique

Founded in 1714, the Opéra Comique is one of the oldest theatrical institutions in Paris. It specializes in opéra comique, a genre that combines spoken dialogue with music. The beautiful Salle Favart, where performances are held, is a historic venue that offers a unique cultural experience.

Catch a Show at the Grand Rex

The Grand Rex, an iconic cinema and concert hall, is the largest in Europe. Its Art Deco architecture and grand interior make it a must-visit. The venue hosts a variety of events, including film screenings, concerts, and live performances. The annual Christmas show is particularly popular with families.

Famous Places

The 2nd Arrondissement is home to several notable landmarks and attractions that reflect its rich history and cultural significance.

Palais Brongniart (Bourse)

The Palais Brongniart, designed by architect Alexandre-Théodore Brongniart, is an architectural gem that once housed the Paris Stock Exchange. While the stock exchange has moved, the building remains a symbol of the arrondissement's financial heritage. Today, it serves as an event space, hosting conferences, exhibitions, and other public events.

Place des Victoires

Place des Victoires is one of the oldest royal squares in Paris, created in 1686 to honor King Louis XIV's military victories. The centerpiece of the square is an equestrian statue of Louis XIV, designed by François Joseph Bosio in 1828 after the original statue was destroyed during the French Revolution. The elegant, circular square is surrounded by classical buildings and exudes a regal atmosphere.

Basilica of Notre-Dame des Victoires

Located near Place des Victoires, the Basilica of Notre-Dame des Victoires is a beautiful Baroque church built in the 17th century. It is known for its stunning interior, including intricate carvings, stained glass windows, and a magnificent organ. The church has a rich history and has been a place of pilgrimage for centuries, attracting visitors with its serene and spiritual ambiance.

Rue Réaumur

Rue Réaumur is a notable street famous for its distinctive architecture. The buildings along this street were constructed in the late 19th and early 20th centuries and are characterized by their ornate facades and decorative elements. Walking down Rue Réaumur offers a glimpse into the architectural trends of the Belle Époque era and the early 20th century.

Tour Jean Sans Peur

The Tour Jean Sans Peur (Tower of John Without Fear) is a medieval tower that once formed part of the grand residence of the Dukes of Burgundy. Built in the early 15th century, it is one of the few remaining examples of medieval architecture in Paris. The tower is open to the public and offers a fascinating look into the history and daily life of the medieval aristocracy.

What to Eat and Famous Restaurants

The 2nd Arrondissement is a food lover's paradise, offering a diverse range of dining experiences. From traditional French cuisine to international flavors, there's something to satisfy every palate.

Le Grand Colbert

Le Grand Colbert is a classic Parisian brasserie that exudes old-world charm. Known for its Art Deco interior and traditional French menu, it offers dishes such as escargots, foie gras, and duck confit. The restaurant gained international fame when it was featured in the film "Something's Gotta Give." Dining here is like stepping back in time to the Belle Époque era.

Frenchie

Frenchie is a trendy and highly acclaimed restaurant that has become a favorite among locals and tourists alike. Helmed by chef Gregory Marchand, the restaurant offers a modern twist on French cuisine, with a focus on fresh, seasonal ingredients. The menu changes frequently, reflecting the chef's creativity and the availability of local produce. Reservations are essential due to its popularity.

L'Escargot Montorgueil

For a quintessentially Parisian dining experience, visit L'Escargot Montorgueil. Established in 1832, this charming restaurant specializes in escargot, offering a variety of preparations of the famous French delicacy. The interior is adorned with Belle Époque decor, making it a delightful place to enjoy a meal.

Le Bouillon Chartier

Although technically located in the 9th Arrondissement, Le Bouillon Chartier is within walking distance of the 2nd and is worth the detour. This historic restaurant, founded in 1896, serves traditional French fare in a lively, bustling atmosphere. The menu is extensive and affordable, making it a great spot to enjoy classic dishes such as steak frites, coq au vin, and crème brûlée.

Rue Montorgueil

Rue Montorgueil is not only a great place for shopping but also for dining. The street is lined with a variety of cafes, bistros, and specialty food shops. Some notable spots include:

- **Stohrer:** One of the oldest patisseries in Paris, Stohrer was founded in 1730 and is famous for its pastries, including the iconic baba au rhum.
- **L'Escargot Montorgueil:** As mentioned earlier, this historic restaurant is a must-visit for escargot lovers.
- **Le Compas:** A classic Parisian bistro offering a range of traditional dishes in a relaxed, welcoming setting.

Experimental Cocktail Club

For a sophisticated evening out, visit the Experimental Cocktail Club. This stylish speakeasy-style bar offers expertly crafted cocktails in an intimate and chic atmosphere. The menu features a variety of creative concoctions, and the bartenders are known for their mixology skills. It's a perfect spot for a pre-dinner drink or a nightcap.

Summary

The 2nd Arrondissement of Paris, also known as Bourse, is a vibrant and historically rich area that offers a unique blend of old and new. Its history as a commercial and financial hub is reflected in its landmarks, such as the Palais Brongniart and the elegant covered passages. These passages, like Passage des Panoramas and Galerie Vivienne, provide a charming glimpse into 19th-century Parisian life and remain popular shopping and dining destinations.

3RD ARRONDISSEMENT (TEMPLE)

Main Interesting History Facts of the Arrondissement

The 3rd Arrondissement, also known as Temple, is one of the oldest areas in Paris, rich in historical significance and cultural heritage. Its name derives from the Knights Templar, whose medieval headquarters were located here.

The Knights Templar

The history of the 3rd Arrondissement is closely linked to the Knights Templar, a medieval Christian military order. In the 12th century, they established their European headquarters in this area, building the Temple Church and a massive fortress known as the Temple Tower. The Templars amassed great wealth and influence, but they were eventually disbanded in the early 14th century under the orders of King Philip IV of France. The remnants of their presence, particularly the Temple Tower, became an infamous prison during the French Revolution, where King Louis XVI and his family were held before their execution.

The Marais District

The Marais, a historic district that spans the 3rd and 4th Arrondissements, was once a swampy area that was drained and developed in the Middle Ages. By the 17th century, it had become a fashionable neighborhood for the French nobility, who built grand hôtels particuliers (private mansions) here. Many of these elegant buildings still stand today, housing museums, art galleries, and cultural institutions.

The Jewish Quarter

The 3rd Arrondissement is also home to one of Paris's oldest Jewish communities. The Pletzl (Yiddish for "little place") in the Marais has been a center of Jewish life since the 13th century. Despite periods of persecution and upheaval, the Jewish community has remained resilient, and the area is known for its kosher bakeries, delis, and synagogues. Rue des Rosiers is the heart of this vibrant Jewish quarter.

The French Revolution

During the French Revolution, the 3rd Arrondissement was a hotbed of revolutionary activity. The Temple Tower and other local landmarks played significant roles during this tumultuous period. The area's narrow streets and dense population made it a focal point for revolutionary fervor and political gatherings.

Modern Times

In recent decades, the 3rd Arrondissement has undergone significant gentrification, transforming into a trendy and desirable neighborhood. It is now known for its vibrant cultural scene, with numerous museums, art galleries, boutiques, and cafes. The mix of historic charm and modern amenities makes it a popular destination for both locals and tourists.

Things To Do You Can't Miss

The 3rd Arrondissement offers a wealth of activities and attractions that cater to a variety of interests. Whether you're a history buff, an art enthusiast, or a foodie, there's something for everyone.

Visit the Musée Picasso

The Musée Picasso, housed in the stunning Hôtel Salé, is a must-visit for art lovers. The museum boasts one of the world's largest collections of works by Pablo Picasso, including paintings, sculptures, drawings, and ceramics. The collection spans Picasso's entire career, offering a comprehensive look at his artistic evolution. The building itself is a masterpiece of 17th-century architecture, adding to the museum's allure.

Explore the Musée des Arts et Métiers

The Musée des Arts et Métiers is an industrial design and technology museum that showcases the history of inventions and innovations. Housed in the former priory of Saint-Martin-des-Champs, the museum's collection includes scientific instruments, early machines, and models of groundbreaking inventions. Highlights include Foucault's pendulum and a reconstruction of the first airplane.

Wander Through the Marché des Enfants Rouges

The Marché des Enfants Rouges is the oldest covered market in Paris, dating back to 1615. It's a bustling and vibrant market where you can sample a variety of international cuisines, from Moroccan tagines to Japanese bento boxes. The market also offers fresh produce, flowers, and gourmet products. It's a great place to enjoy a casual meal or pick up ingredients for a picnic.

Stroll Along Rue des Rosiers

Rue des Rosiers is the heart of the Jewish quarter in the Marais. This lively street is lined with kosher bakeries, delis, and shops selling traditional Jewish goods. It's a great place to try some authentic Jewish cuisine, such as falafel from the famous L'As du Fallafel or a pastry from Sacha Finkelsztajn's bakery. The street is also home to several historic synagogues and cultural sites.

Discover the Archives Nationales

The Archives Nationales, located in the Hôtel de Soubise and the Hôtel de Rohan, house important documents and records from French history. The archives are open to the public, and visitors can explore exhibitions that showcase historical documents, maps, and artifacts. The buildings themselves are architectural gems, with beautifully preserved interiors and gardens.

Famous Places

The 3rd Arrondissement is home to several notable landmarks and attractions that reflect its rich history and cultural significance.

Place des Vosges

Although technically located in the 4th Arrondissement, Place des Vosges straddles the border with the 3rd and is an essential part of the Marais district. This elegant square, built by Henri IV in the early 17th century, is the oldest planned square in Paris. Its perfectly symmetrical layout, red brick facades, and arcaded walkways make it a quintessential example of early French urban planning. The square is surrounded by stunning hôtels particuliers, including the Maison de Victor Hugo, where the famous writer lived and which is now a museum dedicated to his life and works.

Musée Carnavalet

The Musée Carnavalet, dedicated to the history of Paris, is located in two historic mansions—the Hôtel Carnavalet and the Hôtel Le Peletier de Saint-Fargeau. The museum's extensive collection includes artifacts, paintings, sculptures, and decorative arts that chronicle the city's history from its origins to the present day.

Highlights include items from the French Revolution, such as the keys to the Bastille and revolutionary pamphlets. The museum's beautiful gardens and period rooms offer a delightful glimpse into Parisian life through the ages.

Carreau du Temple

The Carreau du Temple, originally a covered market built in the 19th century, has been transformed into a vibrant cultural and sports center. The building's stunning iron and glass architecture has been preserved, and it now hosts a variety of events, including fashion shows, concerts, exhibitions, and markets. It's also home to sports facilities where visitors can participate in activities like yoga, boxing, and dance.

Hôtel de Saint-Aignan

The Hôtel de Saint-Aignan is another beautiful mansion in the Marais, dating back to the 17th century. It now houses the Musée d'Art et d'Histoire du Judaïsme, dedicated to Jewish art and history. The museum's collection includes religious artifacts, historical documents, and works of art that trace the history and culture of Jewish communities in France and around the world. The building itself is an architectural gem, with a stunning courtyard and elegant interiors.

Square du Temple

Square du Temple is a charming public garden located on the site of the former Templar fortress. The garden features a picturesque pond, lush greenery, and a variety of plant species, making it a peaceful oasis in the heart of the city. It's a great place to relax, take a leisurely walk, or enjoy a picnic. The garden also has a children's playground and hosts occasional cultural events.

What to Eat and Famous Restaurants

The 3rd Arrondissement is a food lover's paradise, offering a diverse array of dining options, from traditional French cuisine to international fare.

Breizh Café

Breizh Café is a beloved creperie that offers some of the best crêpes and galettes in Paris. The menu features a variety of savory and sweet options, all made with high-quality ingredients sourced from

Brittany. Don't miss the classic galette complète, filled with ham, cheese, and a sunny-side-up egg, or the indulgent caramel beurre salé crêpe for dessert. The café also has an impressive selection of ciders to complement your meal.

L'As du Fallafel

L'As du Fallafel, located on Rue des Rosiers, is an iconic eatery famous for its delicious and generous falafel sandwiches. This bustling spot is a must-visit for anyone exploring the Jewish quarter. The falafel is crispy on the outside, tender on the inside, and served with a medley of fresh vegetables and creamy tahini sauce in a warm pita. It's a perfect option for a quick and satisfying meal.

Le Mary Celeste

Le Mary Celeste is a trendy bar and restaurant known for its inventive small plates and creative cocktails. The menu features a mix of French and international flavors, with dishes that change regularly based on seasonal ingredients. Highlights include fresh oysters, ceviche, and other seafood delicacies. The relaxed atmosphere and stylish decor make it a great spot for a laid-back meal or drinks with friends.

Les Enfants Rouges

Les Enfants Rouges is a charming bistro located near the Marché des Enfants Rouges. The restaurant offers a menu of modern French cuisine with a touch of Japanese influence, reflecting the chef's diverse culinary background. The dishes are beautifully presented and feature fresh, seasonal ingredients. The cozy, intimate setting and friendly service make it a favorite among locals and visitors alike.

Café Charlot

Café Charlot is a classic Parisian brasserie with a lively atmosphere and a prime location near the Marché des Enfants Rouges. The café serves a variety of French dishes, from croque-monsieurs and salads to steak frites and tartare. It's a great place to enjoy a leisurely brunch, lunch, or dinner while people-watching from the outdoor terrace.

Le Sancerre

Le Sancerre is a traditional French bistro that offers a warm and welcoming atmosphere. The menu features classic French dishes such as escargots, beef bourguignon, and crème brûlée. The wine list is extensive, with a focus on wines from the Sancerre region, making it an excellent place to explore French wine pairings. The cozy interior and friendly staff make it a wonderful spot for a relaxed meal.

Dessance

Dessance offers a unique dining experience focused on desserts and innovative cuisine. The restaurant's concept revolves around creating dishes that blur the lines between sweet and savory. The tasting menu features a series of beautifully crafted courses that highlight the chef's creativity and skill. Dessance is perfect for those looking to try something different and indulge in a culinary adventure.

Café des Musées

Café des Musées is a quaint bistro known for its classic French fare and charming atmosphere. Located near the Musée Picasso, it's a great spot for a meal after a visit to the museum. The menu includes traditional dishes such as onion soup, duck confit, and tarte Tatin. The bistro's welcoming ambiance and attentive service make it a favorite among both locals and tourists.

Summary

The 3rd Arrondissement of Paris, known as Temple, is a captivating blend of historical richness and modern vibrancy. Its deep-rooted history, from the medieval era of the Knights Templar to its role in the French Revolution, adds a layer of intrigue to its charming streets and historic buildings. The Marais district, straddling the 3rd and 4th Arrondissements, is particularly noteworthy for its well-preserved hôtels particuliers, vibrant Jewish quarter, and dynamic cultural scene.

Visitors can explore an array of fascinating museums, such as the Musée Picasso and the Musée Carnavalet, which offer insights into the artistic and historical heritage of Paris. The bustling Marché des Enfants Rouges provides a delightful culinary experience, while Rue des Rosiers offers a taste of Jewish culture and cuisine. The arrondissement's cultural venues, like the Carreau du Temple, and public spaces, such as Square du Temple, add to the area's appeal.

The 3rd Arrondissement also boasts a diverse culinary landscape, from traditional French bistros to innovative dining concepts. Whether you're savoring crêpes at Breizh Café, enjoying falafel at L'As du Fallafel, or indulging in the creative dishes at Dessance, there's no shortage of gastronomic delights to discover.

In summary, the 3rd Arrondissement is a vibrant and historically significant part of Paris that offers a unique blend of old-world charm and contemporary allure. Its rich cultural heritage, coupled with its dynamic dining scene and picturesque streets, make it a must-visit destination for anyone exploring the city.

4TH ARRONDISSEMENT (HÔTEL-DE-VILLE)

Main Interesting History Facts of the Arrondissement

The 4th Arrondissement, also known as Hôtel-de-Ville, is one of Paris's most historically rich and culturally vibrant districts. It encompasses the eastern part of the Marais district and the islands of Île de la Cité and Île Saint-Louis, making it a focal point of Parisian history.

Île de la Cité

The Île de la Cité is the historic heart of Paris and one of the city's two natural islands. It has been a strategic site since ancient times, serving as a Roman outpost and later as the political and religious center of medieval Paris. The island is home to the iconic Notre-Dame Cathedral, the Sainte-Chapelle with its stunning stained glass windows, and the Conciergerie, a former royal palace and prison where Marie Antoinette was held before her execution.

Hôtel de Ville

The Hôtel de Ville, the city hall of Paris, is an architectural masterpiece and a symbol of the city's governance. The original building was constructed in the 14th century, but it was rebuilt in the Renaissance style during the 16th century. After being burned down during the Paris Commune of 1871, it was reconstructed in its current form, combining neo-Renaissance elements with modern amenities. The Hôtel de Ville has been the site of numerous significant events, including political rallies, celebrations, and public gatherings.

The Marais District

The 4th Arrondissement encompasses the eastern part of the Marais district, renowned for its well-preserved medieval and Renaissance architecture. The Marais has a rich history as a center of Jewish life, particularly around Rue des Rosiers, and as a fashionable neighborhood for the French nobility in the 17th century. The area is dotted with grand hôtels particuliers, including the Hôtel de Sully and the Hôtel Carnavalet, which now houses the Musée Carnavalet dedicated to the history of Paris.

The French Revolution

The 4th Arrondissement played a significant role during the French Revolution. The storming of the Bastille prison, a pivotal event that marked the beginning of the revolution, took place just outside the current boundaries of the arrondissement. The area was also home to many revolutionary clubs and gatherings, contributing to the radical changes that reshaped France.

Île Saint-Louis

Île Saint-Louis, the smaller of the two natural islands in the Seine, is a tranquil and picturesque neighborhood known for its elegant 17th-century townhouses. Unlike Île de la Cité, which has been a center of activity since ancient times, Île Saint-Louis was developed in the early 17th century as a residential area for the Parisian elite. Today, it retains a timeless charm with its narrow streets, boutique shops, and artisanal ice cream parlors like the famous Berthillon.

Things To Do You Can't Miss

The 4th Arrondissement offers a wealth of activities and attractions that cater to a variety of interests. Whether you're drawn to historical landmarks, cultural institutions, or simply enjoying the ambiance of Parisian streets, there's something for everyone.

Visit Notre-Dame Cathedral

Notre-Dame Cathedral, a masterpiece of French Gothic architecture, is one of the most famous landmarks in Paris. Despite the devastating fire in April 2019, which severely damaged the roof and spire, the cathedral remains a symbol of resilience and faith. Visitors can admire its stunning facade, intricate sculptures, and the iconic gargoyles. The ongoing restoration efforts aim to restore the cathedral to its former glory, and the plaza in front of Notre-Dame offers a panoramic view of the Seine and the surrounding area.

Explore the Sainte-Chapelle

The Sainte-Chapelle, located within the Palais de la Cité, is renowned for its breathtaking stained glass windows that depict biblical scenes in vivid color. Built in the 13th century by King Louis IX to house his collection of Passion relics, the chapel is a stunning example of Rayonnant Gothic architecture. The upper chapel, with its towering stained glass walls, is a must-see for any visitor to Paris.

Walk Along the Seine

A leisurely walk along the Seine River is one of the most enjoyable ways to experience the beauty of Paris. The 4th Arrondissement offers some of the best riverfront promenades, with picturesque views of historic bridges, charming quays, and iconic landmarks. The pedestrian-friendly paths are perfect for a relaxing stroll, a romantic walk, or simply soaking in the Parisian atmosphere.

Visit the Musée Carnavalet

The Musée Carnavalet, dedicated to the history of Paris, is located in two historic mansions in the Marais district. The museum's extensive collection includes artifacts, paintings, sculptures, and decorative arts that chronicle the city's history from its origins to the present day. The beautifully preserved period rooms and the elegant gardens offer a fascinating glimpse into Parisian life through the ages.

Discover Place des Vosges

Place des Vosges, one of the oldest and most beautiful squares in Paris, is located at the border of the 3rd and 4th Arrondissements in the Marais district. Built by Henri IV in the early 17th century, it features perfectly symmetrical red-brick buildings, arcades, and lush gardens. The square is surrounded by elegant hôtels particuliers and is a perfect spot for a leisurely stroll, a picnic, or simply enjoying the serene ambiance. The Maison de Victor Hugo, located at No. 6 Place des Vosges, is now a museum dedicated to the famous writer.

Visit the Centre Pompidou

The Centre Pompidou, also known as the Beaubourg, is a cultural complex and modern art museum that stands out with its distinctive high-tech architecture. Designed by Renzo Piano and Richard Rogers, the building's colorful exterior exposes its structural elements, making it an architectural icon. Inside, the Musée National d'Art Moderne houses one of the largest collections of modern and contemporary art in Europe, featuring works by Picasso, Matisse, Duchamp, and many others. The center also hosts temporary exhibitions, a public library, and a rooftop terrace with panoramic views of Paris.

Explore the Jewish Quarter

The Jewish Quarter, centered around Rue des Rosiers in the Marais district, is a vibrant area steeped in history and culture. It is home to numerous kosher bakeries, delis, and restaurants, as well as shops selling Judaica and other unique items. The area's rich cultural heritage is reflected in its synagogues and the presence of the Shoah Memorial, which commemorates the victims of the Holocaust and provides insights into Jewish history and culture.

Wander Through Île Saint-Louis

Île Saint-Louis offers a quaint and picturesque escape from the bustling city. The island's narrow streets are lined with charming boutiques, art galleries, and cafés. One of the island's highlights is the famous Berthillon ice cream parlor, known for its artisanal ice creams and sorbets. The peaceful ambiance and beautiful views of the Seine make Île Saint-Louis a delightful place to explore.

Visit the Shoah Memorial

The Shoah Memorial, located in the Marais district, is a moving tribute to the victims of the Holocaust. It includes a wall of names inscribed with those who were deported from France during World War II, as well as an underground crypt and a museum with exhibits documenting the history of the Holocaust. The memorial serves as a place of remembrance and education, ensuring that the atrocities of the past are never forgotten.

What to Eat and Famous Restaurants

The 4th Arrondissement is a culinary hotspot, offering a diverse array of dining options that range from traditional French cuisine to international flavors. Here are some notable places to eat:

L'As du Fallafel

Located on Rue des Rosiers, L'As du Fallafel is an iconic eatery famous for its delicious and generous falafel sandwiches. The crispy falafel, fresh vegetables, and creamy tahini sauce served in warm pita bread make it a must-visit spot for a quick and satisfying meal. The bustling atmosphere and long lines are a testament to its popularity.

Le Saint-Régis

Le Saint-Régis, located on Île Saint-Louis, is a charming Parisian bistro known for its classic French dishes and cozy ambiance. The menu features favorites such as onion soup, steak frites, and duck confit. Its prime location and inviting decor make it a great place for a leisurely meal or a coffee break.

Au Bourguignon du Marais

Au Bourguignon du Marais is a traditional French restaurant specializing in cuisine from the Burgundy region. The menu includes hearty dishes such as beef bourguignon, escargots, and coq au vin, all prepared with authentic recipes and high-quality ingredients. The rustic decor and friendly service add to the dining experience.

Chez Julien

Chez Julien is an elegant brasserie located near the Seine, in a beautiful Belle Époque building. The restaurant offers a refined dining experience with a menu that includes classic French dishes such as foie gras, sole meunière, and tarte Tatin. The romantic setting and picturesque views make it a perfect choice for a special occasion.

Berthillon

Berthillon, on Île Saint-Louis, is famous for its artisanal ice creams and sorbets. Using natural ingredients and traditional methods, Berthillon offers a wide range of flavors that are beloved by locals and tourists alike. A visit to Berthillon is a must for any ice cream enthusiast.

Le Loir dans la Théière

Le Loir dans la Théière is a cozy tea salon in the Marais district, known for its delicious pastries and relaxed atmosphere. The café offers a variety of teas, coffees, and homemade cakes, including its famous lemon meringue pie. It's a great spot for a leisurely afternoon tea or a light lunch.

Summary

The 4th Arrondissement, or Hôtel-de-Ville, is a dynamic and historically significant area that offers a unique blend of Parisian charm and cultural richness. From the majestic Notre-Dame

Cathedral to the avant-garde Centre Pompidou, the arrondissement is brimming with iconic landmarks and hidden gems. Its streets are alive with history, art, and culinary delights, making it one of the most alluring neighborhoods in Paris.

Main Attractions

- **Notre-Dame Cathedral:** This Gothic masterpiece, though currently under restoration, remains a symbol of Paris. Its stunning architecture and storied past draw millions of visitors each year.
- **Sainte-Chapelle:** Known for its magnificent stained glass windows, this chapel is a jewel of Gothic architecture.
- **Hôtel de Ville:** The grand city hall of Paris, an architectural marvel with a rich history.
- **Place des Vosges:** The oldest planned square in Paris, offering a serene oasis with its symmetrical architecture and lush gardens.
- **Centre Pompidou:** A hub of modern art and culture, featuring an extensive collection of contemporary artworks.
- **Musée Carnavalet:** Dedicated to the history of Paris, this museum offers fascinating insights through its extensive collections.
- **Île Saint-Louis:** A charming island with quaint streets, boutique shops, and the famous Berthillon ice cream parlor.
- **Shoah Memorial:** A poignant site honoring the victims of the Holocaust, offering educational exhibits and a place of remembrance.

Culinary Highlights

The 4th Arrondissement boasts an eclectic mix of dining options that reflect its diverse cultural influences:

- **L'As du Fallafel:** A must-visit for its renowned falafel sandwiches.
- **Le Saint-Régis:** A classic Parisian bistro offering traditional French fare in a cozy setting.

- **Au Bourguignon du Marais:** Specializing in hearty dishes from the Burgundy region, this restaurant is perfect for lovers of traditional French cuisine.
- **Chez Julien:** An elegant brasserie with a romantic ambiance and refined menu.
- **Berthillon:** Famous for its artisanal ice creams and sorbets, a treat not to be missed.
- **Le Loir dans la Théière:** A charming tea salon known for its delicious pastries and relaxed vibe.

5TH ARRONDISSEMENT (PANTHÉON)

Main Interesting History Facts of the 5th Arrondissement

The 5th Arrondissement, also known as the Panthéon, is one of the oldest and most historically significant areas in Paris. Often referred to as the Latin Quarter due to its historical association with Latin-speaking students, the arrondissement is a hub of academic and intellectual activity.

Roman Lutetia

The 5th Arrondissement is the site of the ancient Roman city of Lutetia. The remains of the Roman era can still be seen today in the form of the Arènes de Lutèce, a Roman amphitheater dating back to the 1st century AD, and the Thermes de Cluny, the ruins of Roman baths that are part of the Musée de Cluny.

The Sorbonne

The arrondissement is home to the Sorbonne, one of the world's oldest and most prestigious universities. Founded in 1257 by Robert de Sorbon, the university became a major center of theological and philosophical thought in the Middle Ages. The Latin Quarter's name comes from the scholarly use of Latin in the area.

The Panthéon

Originally conceived as a church dedicated to St. Genevieve, the Panthéon was transformed during the French Revolution into a mausoleum for eminent French citizens. It houses the remains of notable figures such as Voltaire, Rousseau, Victor Hugo, and Marie Curie. The building itself is a masterpiece of neoclassical architecture.

Literary and Intellectual Hub

The 5th Arrondissement has long been a center for writers, philosophers, and intellectuals. Famous literary figures such as Ernest Hemingway, James Joyce, and Jean-Paul Sartre frequented the area, contributing to its reputation as a vibrant intellectual hub. The renowned Shakespeare and Company bookstore, a haven for English-speaking writers and readers, continues this tradition.

Revolutionary History

The arrondissement played a significant role during the French Revolution. The Panthéon itself, initially intended as a church, was secularized and used to honor revolutionary heroes. The area was also a hotbed of political activity and revolutionary fervor, with many significant events and gatherings taking place in its streets and buildings.

Things To Do You Can't Miss

The 5th Arrondissement offers a rich tapestry of historical sites, cultural attractions, and charming spots that are essential for any visitor to Paris.

Visit the Panthéon

A visit to the Panthéon is a must. This grand neoclassical building is not only an architectural marvel but also a significant historical site. Explore the crypt to pay homage to some of France's greatest minds and enjoy the panoramic views of Paris from the dome.

Explore the Jardin des Plantes

The Jardin des Plantes is a beautiful botanical garden that offers a peaceful escape from the bustling city. It includes a zoo, greenhouses, and the National Museum of Natural History. The garden is perfect for a leisurely stroll among a diverse collection of plants and flowers.

Discover the Arènes de Lutèce

Step back in time by visiting the Arènes de Lutèce, one of the most important remnants of Roman Paris. This ancient amphitheater once hosted gladiatorial combats and theatrical performances. Today, it's a serene park where you can sit and imagine the spectacles of ancient Rome.

Visit the Musée de Cluny

The Musée de Cluny, or the National Museum of the Middle Ages, is housed in a stunning medieval building that incorporates Roman baths. The museum's collection includes the famous "The Lady and the Unicorn" tapestries, medieval artifacts, and Gothic sculptures.

Wander Through Rue Mouffetard

Rue Mouffetard is one of the oldest streets in Paris, known for its lively atmosphere and vibrant market. The street is lined with charming shops, cafés, and restaurants. It's the perfect place to experience the local culture and enjoy some delicious French food.

Explore the Sorbonne and the Latin Quarter

Take a walk around the historic Sorbonne University and the surrounding Latin Quarter. This area is steeped in academic history and boasts a lively student atmosphere. Be sure to visit the beautiful Place de la Sorbonne and the nearby bookstores and cafés.

Visit Shakespeare and Company

Shakespeare and Company is a legendary English-language bookstore located on the banks of the Seine. Founded by American George Whitman in 1951, it has become a literary landmark. The bookstore frequently hosts readings and events and offers a cozy, bookish atmosphere.

What to Eat and Famous Restaurants

The 5th Arrondissement is a food lover's paradise, offering a wide range of culinary delights from traditional French cuisine to international flavors.

Le Coupe-Chou

Le Coupe-Chou is a charming restaurant set in a series of 17th-century buildings. It offers a cozy, rustic atmosphere and a menu of classic French dishes such as duck confit, escargots, and crème brûlée. The intimate setting and historical ambiance make it a perfect spot for a romantic dinner.

La Tour d'Argent

La Tour d'Argent is one of Paris' most famous and historic restaurants. Established in 1582, it is known for its stunning views of the Seine and Notre-Dame Cathedral, as well as its legendary pressed duck. With a rich history and a Michelin star, dining at La Tour d'Argent is a quintessential Parisian experience.

Le Pré Verre

Le Pré Verre is a contemporary bistro offering innovative French cuisine at reasonable prices. The menu changes regularly, featuring seasonal ingredients and creative combinations. The relaxed atmosphere and excellent wine selection make it a favorite among locals and visitors alike.

L'Ébauchoir

L'Ébauchoir is a charming bistro known for its warm ambiance and delicious traditional French dishes. The menu includes classics such as beef tartare, roasted lamb, and crème caramel. The friendly service and cozy setting make it a great choice for a satisfying meal.

Café de Flore

Although technically located in the 6th Arrondissement, Café de Flore is worth a mention due to its proximity and historical significance in the Latin Quarter. This iconic café has been a gathering place for intellectuals and artists since the early 20th century. Enjoy a coffee or a light meal while soaking in the rich literary history.

Les Pipos

Les Pipos is a traditional Parisian bistro offering hearty French cuisine in a convivial atmosphere. The menu features dishes like coq au vin, beef bourguignon, and tarte Tatin. The lively ambiance and friendly staff make it a popular spot for both locals and tourists.

La Petite Périgourdine

La Petite Périgourdine is a cozy restaurant specializing in cuisine from the Périgord region of France. The menu includes foie gras, duck confit, and cassoulet, all prepared with authentic recipes and high-quality ingredients. The rustic decor and warm service add to the dining experience.

Le Petit Pontoise

Le Petit Pontoise is a charming bistro located near the Seine, offering a menu of classic French dishes with a modern twist. The cozy interior and attentive service create a welcoming atmosphere. Popular dishes include the lamb shank, scallops, and chocolate fondant.

Summary

The 5th Arrondissement, or Panthéon, is a treasure trove of history, culture, and culinary delights. From its ancient Roman roots to its vibrant intellectual scene, the arrondissement offers a unique blend of old and new. Visitors can explore iconic landmarks like the Panthéon and the Sorbonne, wander through the picturesque Jardin des Plantes, and indulge in delicious meals at some of Paris' finest restaurants. The area's rich heritage and lively atmosphere make it a must-visit destination for anyone seeking to experience the heart and soul of Paris.

6TH ARRONDISSEMENT (LUXEMBOURG)

Main Interesting History Facts of the 6th Arrondissement

The 6th Arrondissement, also known as Luxembourg, is one of Paris' most charming and culturally rich neighborhoods. It is renowned for its beautiful gardens, intellectual heritage, and vibrant art scene.

The Luxembourg Palace and Gardens

The Luxembourg Palace, commissioned by Marie de' Medici in the early 17th century, has a fascinating history. Originally built as a royal residence, it now houses the French Senate. The surrounding Luxembourg Gardens, designed in the Italian style, are among the most beautiful and popular parks in Paris, featuring statues, fountains, and meticulously maintained lawns.

Saint-Germain-des-Prés

Saint-Germain-des-Prés is one of Paris' oldest neighborhoods, named after the Abbey of Saint-Germain-des-Prés, founded in the 6th century. This area became a hub of intellectual and artistic activity in the 20th century, frequented by famous writers, philosophers, and artists such as Jean-Paul Sartre, Simone de Beauvoir, and Pablo Picasso.

Café Society

The 6th Arrondissement is synonymous with the café culture that flourished in the early 20th century. Iconic cafés like Café de Flore and Les Deux Magots were meeting places for intellectuals and artists. These establishments played a significant role in the cultural and intellectual life of Paris, hosting discussions that shaped modern thought.

The École des Beaux-Arts

The École des Beaux-Arts, located in the 6th Arrondissement, is one of France's most prestigious art schools. Founded in 1648, it has trained numerous influential artists, including Edgar Degas, Claude Monet, and Pierre-Auguste Renoir. The school's influence on the art world has been profound, contributing to the development of various artistic movements.

Literary Legacy

The arrondissement has a rich literary history, with many renowned authors having lived and worked in the area. The neighborhood's bookshops, such as the famous La Hune, and its proximity to the Sorbonne University have made it a literary hub. The area continues to attract writers and book lovers from around the world.

Things To Do You Can't Miss

The 6th Arrondissement offers a plethora of activities that highlight its historical, cultural, and aesthetic appeal.

Stroll Through Luxembourg Gardens

One of the most enchanting spots in Paris, the Luxembourg Gardens are perfect for a leisurely stroll, a picnic, or simply relaxing by the beautiful Medici Fountain. The gardens also feature a playground, tennis courts, and an orchard, making it a great destination for families.

Visit the Luxembourg Palace

While the interior of the Luxembourg Palace is not regularly open to the public, you can admire its stunning exterior and learn about its history. During certain times of the year, guided tours may be available, offering a closer look at this important political building.

Explore Saint-Germain-des-Prés

Wander through the historic Saint-Germain-des-Prés neighborhood, visit the Abbey of Saint-Germain-des-Prés, and explore its charming streets filled with bookstores, art galleries, and boutique shops. This area is also home to the oldest church in Paris, Église Saint-Germain-des-Prés.

Enjoy a Coffee at Historic Cafés

No visit to the 6th Arrondissement is complete without stopping by its iconic cafés. Enjoy a coffee or a meal at Café de Flore or Les Deux Magots, where you can soak up the atmosphere and imagine the great minds who once gathered there.

Discover the École des Beaux-Arts

While access to the École des Beaux-Arts is limited, you can still admire its historic buildings and visit its exhibitions, which showcase works by students and alumni. The school's architecture and art collections are a testament to its long-standing influence on the art world.

Visit the Musée Delacroix

Dedicated to the life and work of the Romantic artist Eugène Delacroix, the Musée Delacroix is set in the artist's former apartment and studio. The museum features a collection of his paintings, drawings, and personal artifacts, offering insight into his creative process.

Explore the Art Galleries

The 6th Arrondissement is home to numerous art galleries that feature contemporary and classic works. Wander through the streets and discover a variety of art styles and mediums, from painting and sculpture to photography and mixed media.

What to Eat and Famous Restaurants

The 6th Arrondissement boasts an array of dining options, from traditional French bistros to innovative gourmet restaurants.

Les Deux Magots

One of Paris' most famous cafés, Les Deux Magots has been a meeting place for intellectuals and artists for over a century. Enjoy a coffee, a light meal, or a glass of wine while soaking in the historic ambiance.

Café de Flore

Another iconic café, Café de Flore, offers a classic Parisian experience. Known for its literary history, it serves a variety of traditional French dishes, pastries, and beverages in a charming setting.

Le Procope

Le Procope is the oldest café in Paris, established in 1686. This historic restaurant has hosted numerous famous figures, including Voltaire, Benjamin Franklin, and Napoleon. The menu features classic French cuisine, such as coq au vin, escargots, and crème brûlée, served in an elegant, period-style dining room.

L'Avant Comptoir

L'Avant Comptoir is a popular standing-room-only wine bar and tapas spot located near the Odéon Theatre. It offers a selection of delicious small plates, including charcuterie, cheese, and inventive seasonal dishes, paired with excellent French wines.

Le Comptoir du Relais

Adjacent to L'Avant Comptoir, Le Comptoir du Relais is a bistro helmed by celebrated chef Yves Camdeborde. The menu features a mix of traditional and modern French dishes, with a focus on fresh, high-quality ingredients. Reservations are highly recommended for this popular spot.

La Rotonde

La Rotonde is a classic brasserie that has been a favorite of artists and intellectuals since the early 20th century. Located near Montparnasse, it offers a menu of traditional French fare, including steak frites, onion soup, and seafood platters, served in a lively and historic setting.

Chez Fernand

Chez Fernand is a cozy bistro known for its warm atmosphere and hearty French cuisine. The menu features regional specialties such as duck confit, beef bourguignon, and tarte Tatin. The friendly service and intimate setting make it a great choice for a relaxed meal.

La Cuisine de Philippe

La Cuisine de Philippe is a small, family-run restaurant offering a menu of refined French dishes. Known for its soufflés and attentive service, this charming eatery provides a delightful dining experience in a cozy and welcoming environment.

Summary

The 6th Arrondissement (Luxembourg) is a quintessential Parisian neighborhood that perfectly blends history, culture, and charm. From the lush Luxembourg Gardens and the grand Luxembourg Palace to the intellectual legacy of Saint-Germain-des-Prés, the arrondissement offers a rich tapestry of experiences. Visitors can enjoy iconic cafés, explore historic sites, and savor delicious meals at renowned restaurants. Whether you're wandering through art galleries or relaxing in a beautiful park, the 6th Arrondissement provides a delightful and immersive taste of Parisian life.

7TH ARRONDISSEMENT (PALAIS-BOURBON)

Main Interesting History Facts of the 7th Arrondissement

The 7th Arrondissement, also known as Palais-Bourbon, is one of Paris' most prestigious and historically rich neighborhoods. It is home to some of the city's most iconic landmarks and institutions.

The Eiffel Tower

Perhaps the most recognizable symbol of Paris, the Eiffel Tower was completed in 1889 for the Exposition Universelle (World's Fair). Designed by Gustave Eiffel, it was initially met with criticism but has since become a beloved global icon. Standing at 324 meters, it offers breathtaking views of the city.

The Hôtel des Invalides

The Hôtel des Invalides was commissioned by Louis XIV in 1670 as a hospital and home for wounded soldiers. Today, it houses the Musée de l'Armée (Army Museum) and the tomb of Napoleon Bonaparte. The complex is a stunning example of French Baroque architecture.

The Palais Bourbon

The Palais Bourbon, built in the early 18th century, serves as the seat of the French National Assembly. It was originally the residence of the Duchess of Bourbon, the daughter of Louis XIV. The building's neoclassical façade and grand interiors reflect its importance in French political life.

The Musée d'Orsay

Housed in a former Beaux-Arts railway station, the Musée d'Orsay opened in 1986 and is renowned for its extensive collection of Impressionist and Post-Impressionist masterpieces. The museum includes works by artists such as Monet, Van Gogh, Degas, and Renoir.

The Rodin Museum

The Musée Rodin is dedicated to the works of the famous French sculptor Auguste Rodin. The museum is located in the Hôtel Biron, an 18th-century mansion. Its beautiful gardens display some of Rodin's most famous sculptures, including "The Thinker" and "The Gates of Hell."

Things To Do You Can't Miss

The 7th Arrondissement offers a wealth of activities and sights that showcase its historical and cultural significance.

Visit the Eiffel Tower

No trip to the 7th Arrondissement is complete without visiting the Eiffel Tower. Whether you choose to climb the stairs or take the elevator, the views from the top are spectacular. Be sure to visit at night to see the tower illuminated in a dazzling light show.

Explore the Hôtel des Invalides

Spend a few hours exploring the Hôtel des Invalides. Visit the Musée de l'Armée to learn about French military history and pay your respects at Napoleon's Tomb. The complex also includes the beautiful Église du Dôme, with its striking golden dome.

Discover the Musée d'Orsay

The Musée d'Orsay is a must-visit for art lovers. Wander through its galleries to admire the incredible collection of 19th- and early 20th-century art, including iconic paintings, sculptures, and decorative arts. The museum's architecture is also a highlight.

Wander Through the Rodin Museum and Gardens

The Musée Rodin offers a serene escape in the heart of Paris. Explore the mansion's rooms filled with Rodin's sculptures and personal collections, then take a leisurely stroll through the gardens to see his works in a beautiful outdoor setting.

Visit the Palais Bourbon

While the interior of the Palais Bourbon is not regularly open to the public, you can admire its impressive exterior and learn about its history. Guided tours are sometimes available, offering a glimpse into the workings of the French National Assembly.

Stroll Along the Seine

The 7th Arrondissement's location along the Seine River makes it perfect for a scenic walk. Enjoy the views of the river, the bridges, and the beautiful architecture that lines its banks. Don't miss the chance to take a boat tour for a unique perspective of the city.

Explore Rue Cler

Rue Cler is a charming pedestrian street known for its bustling market atmosphere. It is lined with shops, bakeries, cafés, and restaurants, making it an ideal place to experience local Parisian life and sample delicious French food.

What to Eat and Famous Restaurants

The 7th Arrondissement is home to a variety of dining options, from traditional bistros to Michelin-starred restaurants.

Le Jules Verne

Located on the second floor of the Eiffel Tower, Le Jules Verne offers a unique dining experience with stunning views of Paris. The restaurant, led by a Michelin-starred chef, serves elegant French cuisine with a modern twist.

Les Cocottes

Les Cocottes, helmed by renowned chef Christian Constant, offers a relaxed yet refined dining experience. The menu features hearty French dishes served in cast-iron cocottes (casseroles), emphasizing fresh, seasonal ingredients.

L'Ami Jean

L'Ami Jean is a beloved bistro known for its rustic ambiance and Basque-inspired cuisine. The restaurant is famous for its generous portions and friendly atmosphere. Be sure to try their signature rice pudding dessert.

La Fontaine de Mars

La Fontaine de Mars is a classic Parisian brasserie that has been serving traditional French cuisine since 1908. Located near the Eiffel Tower, it offers a charming and authentic dining experience. The menu includes French classics like duck confit, escargots, and crème brûlée. The warm, vintage decor and friendly service make it a beloved spot among locals and tourists alike.

Restaurant David Toutain

Restaurant David Toutain is a Michelin-starred establishment that showcases the innovative cuisine of chef David Toutain. The menu features creative dishes that highlight seasonal and locally sourced ingredients. The minimalist decor and attentive service complement the sophisticated dining experience.

Arpège

Arpège, a three-Michelin-starred restaurant, is run by legendary chef Alain Passard. Known for its focus on vegetables, the restaurant offers exquisite tasting menus that change with the seasons. The elegant setting and impeccable service make it a top destination for fine dining in Paris.

Café Constant

Café Constant is a cozy bistro offering traditional French fare in a casual setting. Owned by chef Christian Constant, the menu includes dishes like beef tartare, roasted chicken, and profiteroles. It's a great place to enjoy a high-quality meal without the formality of fine dining.

Les Ombres

Les Ombres, located on the rooftop of the Musée du Quai Branly, offers spectacular views of the Eiffel Tower and the Paris skyline. The menu features contemporary French cuisine with an emphasis on fresh, seasonal ingredients. The stunning views and stylish decor make it a perfect spot for a romantic dinner or special occasion.

Summary

The 7th Arrondissement (Palais-Bourbon) is one of Paris' most elegant and historically significant neighborhoods. Home to iconic landmarks like the Eiffel Tower, the Hôtel des Invalides, and the Musée d'Orsay, it offers a rich cultural experience. Visitors can explore world-class museums, enjoy scenic walks along the Seine, and indulge in exquisite dining at renowned restaurants. Whether admiring the grandeur of historic buildings or savoring a meal in a charming bistro, the 7th Arrondissement provides a quintessential Parisian experience.

8TH ARRONDISSEMENT (ÉLYSÉE)

Main Interesting History Facts of the 8th Arrondissement

The 8th Arrondissement, also known as Élysée, is one of Paris' most prestigious districts, renowned for its grand boulevards, luxury shops, and significant historical landmarks.

The Champs-Élysées

The Champs-Élysées is arguably the most famous avenue in the world. Stretching from the Place de la Concorde to the Arc de Triomphe, it was originally fields and market gardens until the 17th century when it was transformed into a grand avenue. Today, it is a symbol of Parisian elegance and a major tourist attraction.

The Arc de Triomphe

Commissioned by Napoleon in 1806 after his victory at Austerlitz, the Arc de Triomphe honors those who fought and died for France in the French Revolutionary and Napoleonic Wars. Standing at the western end of the Champs-Élysées, it offers panoramic views of Paris from its observation deck.

The Élysée Palace

The Élysée Palace, built in 1722, has been the official residence of the President of France since 1848. The palace is a stunning example of French neoclassical architecture and has witnessed numerous significant historical events and political decisions.

Place de la Concorde

Place de la Concorde is one of the largest and most famous squares in Paris. It was originally named Place Louis XV and later became the site of the guillotine during the French Revolution, where King Louis XVI and Marie Antoinette were executed. Today, it features the Luxor Obelisk and beautiful fountains.

The Grand Palais and Petit Palais

Constructed for the 1900 Exposition Universelle, the Grand Palais and Petit Palais are architectural masterpieces. The Grand Palais hosts major art exhibitions and events, while the Petit Palais houses the Musée des Beaux-Arts de la Ville de Paris, showcasing fine arts from antiquity to the early 20th century.

51

Things To Do You Can't Miss

The 8th Arrondissement offers a wide range of activities and sights that highlight its historical, cultural, and luxurious appeal.

Stroll Down the Champs-Élysées

A walk along the Champs-Élysées is a must. Enjoy the bustling atmosphere, shop at luxury boutiques, and stop by iconic cafés. The avenue is especially beautiful at night when it is illuminated.

Visit the Arc de Triomphe

Climb to the top of the Arc de Triomphe for a stunning view of Paris. The monument also features an eternal flame that commemorates the Tomb of the Unknown Soldier from World War I.

Explore the Élysée Palace

While the Élysée Palace is not open to the public, you can admire its grand façade from the outside. The palace is occasionally open for special events, such as the European Heritage Days in September.

Discover Place de la Concorde

Take some time to explore Place de la Concorde, with its impressive Luxor Obelisk and elegant fountains. The square offers great photo opportunities and is a significant historical site.

Visit the Grand Palais and Petit Palais

Explore the exhibitions at the Grand Palais, which hosts a variety of art shows and cultural events. Then, head to the Petit Palais to view its extensive art collections for free.

Relax in Parc Monceau

Parc Monceau is a beautiful and tranquil park located in the 8th Arrondissement. It features picturesque English-style gardens, statues, and a variety of plant species. It's a perfect spot for a leisurely stroll or a picnic.

Admire the Madeleine Church

The Madeleine Church, with its grand neoclassical design, resembles a Greek temple. It was completed in 1842 and is dedicated to Mary Magdalene. The interior is equally impressive, with beautiful sculptures and paintings.

What to Eat and Famous Restaurants

The 8th Arrondissement is home to some of Paris' most renowned dining establishments, offering a range of culinary experiences from traditional French cuisine to modern gastronomy.

Le Fouquet's

Le Fouquet's is a legendary Parisian brasserie located on the Champs-Élysées. It has been a favorite among celebrities and politicians since 1899. The menu features classic French dishes such as foie gras, escargots, and steak tartare.

L'Ambroisie

Located in Place des Vosges, L'Ambroisie is a three-Michelin-starred restaurant offering an exquisite dining experience. The cuisine is based on traditional French techniques with a focus on seasonal ingredients. The elegant setting and impeccable service make it a top choice for fine dining.

Pierre Gagnaire

Pierre Gagnaire's eponymous restaurant, located on Rue Balzac, is known for its innovative and artistic approach to French cuisine. With three Michelin stars, the restaurant offers a unique tasting menu that changes with the seasons, highlighting the chef's creativity and expertise.

Le Gabriel

Situated in the luxurious La Réserve Paris Hotel, Le Gabriel is a two-Michelin-starred restaurant that offers a sophisticated dining experience. The menu features contemporary French cuisine crafted by renowned chef Jérôme Banctel. Diners can enjoy exquisitely presented dishes in an opulent, intimate setting.

Le Cinq

Le Cinq, located in the Four Seasons Hotel George V, is a three-Michelin-starred restaurant known for its exceptional service and refined French cuisine. The menu, created by chef Christian Le Squer, includes gourmet dishes that beautifully blend tradition and innovation. The lavish dining room and impeccable attention to detail make it a must-visit for luxury dining.

Epicure

Epicure, housed within the Le Bristol Paris hotel, is a three-Michelin-starred restaurant led by chef Eric Frechon. The restaurant offers a menu of expertly crafted French dishes, with a focus on seasonal ingredients and elegant presentation. The beautiful garden views and luxurious ambiance enhance the dining experience.

Restaurant Laurent

Restaurant Laurent, set in a charming 19th-century pavilion near the Champs-Élysées, offers a serene dining experience with a beautiful terrace. The menu features classic French cuisine with a modern twist, emphasizing fresh, high-quality ingredients. The elegant decor and attentive service make it a popular choice for both lunch and dinner.

Le Relais de l'Entrecôte

Le Relais de l'Entrecôte is a beloved Parisian institution known for its simple yet delicious menu: steak frites. The restaurant serves only one dish—perfectly cooked steak with a secret sauce, accompanied by crispy fries. The bustling atmosphere and consistent quality have made it a favorite among locals and tourists alike.

Summary

The 8th Arrondissement (Élysée) is a district of grandeur and elegance, offering a rich blend of historical landmarks, cultural attractions, and luxurious dining experiences. From the iconic Champs-Élysées and the majestic Arc de Triomphe to the presidential Élysée Palace and the artistic treasures of the Grand Palais and Petit Palais, this arrondissement is a treasure trove of Parisian heritage. Visitors can enjoy leisurely strolls in picturesque parks, indulge in world-class cuisine at Michelin-starred restaurants, and immerse themselves in the vibrant atmosphere of one of Paris' most prestigious neighborhoods. Whether exploring historical sites or savoring gourmet meals, the 8th Arrondissement provides an unforgettable Parisian experience.

9TH ARRONDISSEMENT (OPÉRA)

Main Interesting History Facts of the 9th Arrondissement

The 9th Arrondissement, also known as Opéra, is a vibrant and culturally rich district in Paris, renowned for its theaters, music halls, and historical landmarks.

Palais Garnier

The Palais Garnier, completed in 1875, is one of the most famous opera houses in the world. Designed by architect Charles Garnier in the Beaux-Arts style, it is known for its opulent interiors, grand staircase, and the stunning ceiling painted by Marc Chagall. The opera house inspired Gaston Leroux's novel "The Phantom of the Opera."

Galeries Lafayette and Printemps

Galeries Lafayette and Printemps are two iconic department stores located on Boulevard Haussmann. Established in the late 19th century, these stores are architectural marvels with beautiful glass domes and Art Nouveau facades. They are prime destinations for luxury shopping in Paris.

Musée Grévin

Founded in 1882, the Musée Grévin is one of the oldest wax museums in Europe. It features life-size wax figures of famous personalities from history, politics, arts, and entertainment. The museum's ornate interiors and immersive exhibits make it a popular attraction.

Boulevard des Capucines

Boulevard des Capucines has historical significance as the location of the first public cinema screening by the Lumière brothers in 1895. The boulevard has long been associated with Parisian culture and entertainment, housing numerous theaters and cafés.

Folies Bergère

The Folies Bergère is a historic music hall that opened in 1869. Known for its extravagant variety shows, cabaret performances, and revue productions, it became a symbol of Parisian nightlife and entertainment. Many famous artists, including Josephine Baker, have performed here.

Things To Do You Can't Miss

The 9th Arrondissement offers a wide range of activities and sights that highlight its rich cultural heritage and lively atmosphere.

Visit the Palais Garnier

Take a guided tour of the Palais Garnier to explore its lavish interiors, including the grand foyer, the chandelier-adorned auditorium, and the underground lake that inspired "The Phantom of the Opera." Attend a ballet or opera performance for an unforgettable cultural experience.

Shop at Galeries Lafayette and Printemps

Explore the luxurious Galeries Lafayette and Printemps department stores. Don't miss the stunning glass dome and the rooftop terrace of Galeries Lafayette, which offers panoramic views of Paris. These stores provide an exceptional shopping experience with a wide range of high-end brands.

Explore Musée Grévin

Visit the Musée Grévin to see its impressive collection of wax figures. The museum's interactive exhibits and historical scenes make it an engaging experience for visitors of all ages. Don't forget to take photos with your favorite celebrities and historical figures.

Walk Along Boulevard des Capucines

Stroll down Boulevard des Capucines to soak in the vibrant atmosphere and explore its theaters, shops, and cafés. This historic boulevard is a great place to experience the lively culture of the 9th Arrondissement.

Enjoy a Show at Folies Bergère

Attend a performance at the Folies Bergère to experience the glamour and excitement of Parisian cabaret. The music hall's elaborate productions and talented performers ensure a memorable night of entertainment.

Discover the Square Montholon

Square Montholon is a charming park in the 9th Arrondissement, perfect for a relaxing break. With its beautiful trees, flowerbeds, and statues, it offers a peaceful escape from the bustling city streets.

Visit the Musée de la Vie Romantique

Located in a former artist's home, the Musée de la Vie Romantique is dedicated to the Romantic period in the arts. The museum features artworks, memorabilia, and personal belongings of notable figures like George Sand and Ary Scheffer. The lovely garden café is a perfect spot for a relaxing afternoon.

What to Eat and Famous Restaurants

The 9th Arrondissement is home to a variety of dining options, from traditional bistros to trendy cafés and fine dining establishments.

Le Bouillon Chartier

Le Bouillon Chartier is a historic Parisian brasserie that has been serving affordable French cuisine since 1896. The restaurant's Art Nouveau decor and lively atmosphere make it a popular choice for both locals and tourists. The menu includes classic dishes like escargots, foie gras, and steak frites.

L'Opéra Restaurant

Located within the Palais Garnier, L'Opéra Restaurant offers a unique dining experience in a stunning setting. The menu features contemporary French cuisine with a focus on fresh, seasonal ingredients. The elegant decor and exceptional service make it a perfect choice for a special occasion.

Café de la Paix

Café de la Paix is an iconic Parisian café located near the Palais Garnier. Opened in 1862, it has been a favorite among writers, artists, and politicians. The menu includes traditional French dishes, pastries, and an extensive selection of wines. The beautiful Belle Époque interior and prime location make it an ideal spot for a luxurious meal or a leisurely coffee break.

Le Pantruche

Le Pantruche is a charming bistro offering classic French cuisine in a cozy setting. The menu features dishes like duck confit, escargots, and tarte Tatin, all prepared with a modern twist. The warm ambiance and attentive service have made it a favorite among locals and visitors alike.

Le P'tit Canon

Le P'tit Canon is a traditional Parisian bistro known for its hearty, authentic French dishes. The menu includes a variety of options such as beef bourguignon, coq au vin, and crème brûlée. The casual, rustic atmosphere makes it a great place for a relaxed meal.

Les Canailles

Les Canailles is a contemporary bistro that focuses on seasonal ingredients and inventive dishes. The menu changes regularly, offering fresh takes on classic French cuisine. The intimate setting and friendly service make it a wonderful spot for a romantic dinner or a gathering with friends.

La Taverne de l'Olympia

Located near the famous Olympia music hall, La Taverne de l'Olympia is a lively restaurant offering a mix of French and international dishes. The vibrant atmosphere, live music, and diverse menu make it a popular choice for a fun night out.

Summary

The 9th Arrondissement (Opéra) of Paris is a dynamic and culturally rich district, known for its historic landmarks, vibrant arts scene, and elegant shopping destinations. From the opulent Palais Garnier and the bustling Galeries Lafayette to the lively Folies Bergère and the charming Musée de la Vie Romantique, the arrondissement offers a diverse array of experiences.

Visitors can enjoy world-class performances, explore historic sites, and indulge in both traditional and contemporary French cuisine at renowned restaurants. Whether strolling down the iconic boulevards, relaxing in picturesque parks, or savoring gourmet meals, the 9th Arrondissement provides a quintessentially Parisian experience that beautifully blends history, culture, and modern luxury.

10TH ARRONDISSEMENT (ENTREPÔT)

Main Interesting History Facts of the 10th Arrondissement

The 10th Arrondissement, also known as Entrepôt, is a lively and diverse district in Paris, characterized by its historic canals, bustling train stations, and vibrant multicultural atmosphere.

Canal Saint-Martin

The Canal Saint-Martin, constructed in the early 19th century, was originally designed to supply fresh water to the city and facilitate the transportation of goods. Today, the picturesque canal is a popular spot for leisurely walks, boat rides, and picnics along its tree-lined banks. The iron footbridges and charming locks add to its romantic appeal.

Gare du Nord

Gare du Nord, opened in 1864, is one of the busiest railway stations in Europe and a major hub for international travel. The historic station features an impressive facade adorned with statues representing cities served by the railway. It connects Paris with various destinations across France and Europe, including London via the Eurostar.

Gare de l'Est

Gare de l'Est, another significant railway station in the 10th Arrondissement, was inaugurated in 1849. It served as a departure point for soldiers during World War I, symbolized by the statue "L'Aurore" (The Dawn) on its facade. The station continues to be a vital link for travel to Eastern France and beyond.

Passage Brady

Passage Brady, known as "Little India" of Paris, is a bustling covered market established in 1828. It is famous for its Indian, Pakistani, and Bangladeshi shops and restaurants, offering a vibrant cultural experience. The passage is a testament to the arrondissement's multicultural heritage.

Saint-Vincent-de-Paul Church

Constructed between 1824 and 1844, Saint-Vincent-de-Paul Church is a striking example of neoclassical architecture. The church features two towers, a grand portico with Corinthian columns, and beautiful interior frescoes. It stands as a significant religious and historical landmark in the district.

Things To Do You Can't Miss

The 10th Arrondissement offers a variety of activities and sights that showcase its unique blend of history, culture, and modern urban life.

Stroll Along Canal Saint-Martin

Take a leisurely walk along the Canal Saint-Martin, enjoying the scenic views, quaint bridges, and lively atmosphere. The canal is lined with trendy boutiques, cafés, and restaurants, making it an ideal spot for a relaxing afternoon.

Explore Gare du Nord and Gare de l'Est

Visit Gare du Nord and Gare de l'Est to admire their architectural grandeur and historical significance. Both stations are bustling with activity and offer a glimpse into the dynamic nature of Paris as a major travel hub.

Discover Passage Brady

Wander through Passage Brady to experience the vibrant sights, sounds, and flavors of "Little India." Sample delicious Indian cuisine, browse colorful textiles, and explore the diverse shops that define this unique market.

Enjoy a Boat Ride on Canal Saint-Martin

Embark on a boat ride along the Canal Saint-Martin to see the district from a different perspective. The leisurely cruises often include passing through the canal's locks and under its iconic footbridges, providing a charming and romantic experience.

Visit Saint-Vincent-de-Paul Church

Admire the architectural beauty of Saint-Vincent-de-Paul Church and explore its serene interior. The church's frescoes and neoclassical design elements make it a peaceful retreat in the heart of the bustling arrondissement.

Relax in Jardin Villemin

Jardin Villemin is a lovely park near Gare de l'Est, offering a green oasis amid the urban landscape. With its well-maintained gardens, playgrounds, and picnic areas, it's a perfect spot for a leisurely break or family outing.

Explore the Marché Saint-Quentin

Visit the Marché Saint-Quentin, one of the oldest covered markets in Paris, dating back to 1866. The market offers a wide range of fresh produce, meats, cheeses, and international foods, providing an authentic Parisian shopping experience.

What to Eat and Famous Restaurants

The 10th Arrondissement is home to a diverse culinary scene, with a range of options from traditional French bistros to international eateries reflecting the district's multicultural flair.

Le Verre Volé

Le Verre Volé is a popular wine bar and restaurant located near Canal Saint-Martin. It offers a menu of delicious, seasonal dishes paired with an extensive selection of natural wines. The cozy atmosphere and friendly service make it a favorite among locals and visitors.

Chez Michel

Chez Michel is a traditional French bistro known for its hearty Breton cuisine. The menu features dishes like seafood stew, roasted duck, and tarte Tatin, all made with fresh, high-quality ingredients. The rustic decor and warm ambiance create an inviting dining experience.

Brasserie Flo

Brasserie Flo, housed in a historic building from the 19th century, offers a classic French brasserie experience. The menu includes traditional dishes such as escargots, steak tartare, and seafood platters. The elegant decor, featuring wood paneling and vintage posters, adds to the authentic Parisian atmosphere.

Holybelly

Holybelly is a trendy café and brunch spot near Canal Saint-Martin, known for its delicious breakfast and brunch options. The menu features a mix of international and French dishes, including pancakes, eggs Benedict, and gourmet coffee. The casual, hip ambiance and friendly staff make it a popular spot for locals and tourists.

La Fidélité

La Fidélité is a chic bistro offering a blend of French and fusion cuisine. The menu includes innovative dishes like foie gras burgers and truffle risotto, as well as classic French fare. The stylish interior, with its art deco influences, creates a sophisticated dining experience.

Les Enfants Perdus

Les Enfants Perdus is a charming restaurant near Canal Saint-Martin, offering a menu of contemporary French cuisine. The dishes are crafted with seasonal ingredients and presented beautifully. The cozy, intimate setting, complete with exposed brick walls and warm lighting, makes it perfect for a romantic dinner.

Du Pain et des Idées

Du Pain et des Idées is a renowned bakery known for its artisanal bread and pastries. Located near Canal Saint-Martin, it offers a variety of delicious baked goods, including the famous "escargot" pastries and traditional baguettes. The quality and craftsmanship of the bakery have earned it a loyal following.

Summary

The 10th Arrondissement (Entrepôt) of Paris is a vibrant and eclectic district, offering a unique blend of historical landmarks, cultural diversity, and modern urban charm. From the picturesque Canal Saint-Martin and the bustling Gare du Nord and Gare de l'Est to the lively Passage Brady and the serene Jardin Villemin, the arrondissement is rich in both history and contemporary attractions.

Visitors can enjoy leisurely strolls along the canal, explore the architectural beauty of historic train stations, and immerse themselves in the multicultural atmosphere of local markets and eateries. The area is also home to a diverse culinary scene, with options ranging from traditional French bistros to trendy cafés and international restaurants.

Whether you're looking to relax by the water, discover hidden gems in historic passages, or indulge in delicious food, the 10th

Arrondissement offers an authentic and dynamic Parisian experience that reflects the city's rich cultural tapestry.

11TH ARRONDISSEMENT (POPINCOURT)

Main Interesting History Facts of the 11th Arrondissement

The 11th Arrondissement, also known as Popincourt, is a vibrant and historically significant district in Paris. Known for its revolutionary past, bustling nightlife, and diverse cultural scene, it offers a unique glimpse into Parisian life.

Place de la Bastille

The Place de la Bastille is one of the most historically significant squares in Paris. It was the site of the Bastille prison, stormed on July 14, 1789, marking the beginning of the French Revolution. Today, the July Column stands in the center of the square, commemorating the Revolution of 1830.

Cirque d'Hiver

Opened in 1852, Cirque d'Hiver is one of the oldest circus buildings in the world. Designed by architect Jacques Hittorff, it has hosted a variety of performances, including traditional circus acts, concerts, and fashion shows. The building's ornate facade and rich history make it a notable landmark.

Rue Oberkampf

Rue Oberkampf is a lively street known for its vibrant nightlife and artistic flair. Named after Christophe-Philippe Oberkampf, a renowned textile manufacturer, it became a hub for artists and musicians in the late 20th century. The street is lined with bars, cafés, and music venues, offering a dynamic cultural experience.

Église Saint-Ambroise

Built between 1863 and 1868, Église Saint-Ambroise is a stunning example of neo-Romanesque architecture. The church is dedicated to Saint Ambrose and features beautiful stained glass windows and intricate sculptures. It played a significant role during the social unrest in the late 19th and early 20th centuries.

Faubourg Saint-Antoine

The Faubourg Saint-Antoine is a historic area known for its association with furniture makers and craftsmen. Dating back to the Middle Ages, it was a center for artisans and played a crucial role in the economic development of Paris. Today, it remains a bustling area with shops, workshops, and markets.

Things To Do You Can't Miss

The 11th Arrondissement offers a variety of activities and sights that highlight its rich history, cultural diversity, and vibrant atmosphere.

Visit Place de la Bastille

Explore Place de la Bastille, where you can view the July Column and learn about the historical significance of the Bastille prison. The area is also home to the Opéra Bastille, a modern opera house offering world-class performances.

Enjoy a Show at Cirque d'Hiver

Attend a performance at Cirque d'Hiver to experience the magic of one of the world's oldest circus buildings. The venue hosts a variety of shows, including traditional circus acts, concerts, and special events.

Stroll Along Rue Oberkampf

Take a walk along Rue Oberkampf to soak in the lively atmosphere and discover its vibrant street art, eclectic bars, and trendy cafés. The street is a hub for nightlife, offering a wide range of entertainment options.

Explore Église Saint-Ambroise

Visit Église Saint-Ambroise to admire its beautiful architecture and serene interior. The church's stained glass windows and detailed sculptures make it a peaceful retreat in the midst of the bustling arrondissement.

Discover the Artisanal Shops of Faubourg Saint-Antoine

Wander through the Faubourg Saint-Antoine to explore its artisan workshops, boutiques, and markets. The area is known for its high-quality craftsmanship, particularly in furniture and design.

Relax in Square Maurice Gardette

Square Maurice Gardette is a charming park offering a green oasis in the heart of the 11th Arrondissement. With its well-maintained gardens, playgrounds, and peaceful atmosphere, it's a perfect spot for a leisurely break.

Visit Atelier des Lumières

Atelier des Lumières is a digital art center housed in a former foundry. It offers immersive exhibitions that combine art and technology, projecting famous artworks onto the walls and floors of the space. It's a unique cultural experience that shouldn't be missed.

What to Eat and Famous Restaurants

The 11th Arrondissement boasts a diverse culinary scene, with a range of options from traditional French bistros to innovative eateries and international cuisine.

Septime

Septime is a critically acclaimed restaurant offering a modern take on French cuisine. The menu features seasonal ingredients and inventive dishes, earning it a spot on the list of the world's best restaurants. The minimalist decor and intimate setting enhance the dining experience.

Le Chateaubriand

Le Chateaubriand is a renowned bistro known for its creative and ever-changing menu. Chef Inaki Aizpitarte's innovative approach to French cuisine has earned the restaurant critical acclaim. The casual, lively atmosphere makes it a popular choice for food enthusiasts.

Astier

Astier is a traditional French bistro offering classic dishes like coq au vin, escargots, and cheese platters. The warm, rustic decor and friendly service create an inviting atmosphere that makes it ideal for a comforting and authentic French dining experience.

Le Servan

Le Servan is a modern bistro run by the talented Filipino-French chefs Tatiana and Katia Levha. The menu blends French culinary traditions with Asian influences, resulting in unique and flavorful dishes. The stylish yet relaxed setting and the focus on fresh, high-quality ingredients make it a standout in the 11th Arrondissement.

Clamato

Clamato, a seafood-focused restaurant by the team behind Septime, offers a casual dining experience with an emphasis on fresh, high-quality seafood. The menu changes daily based on seasonal availability, featuring dishes like oysters, ceviche, and seafood platters. The cozy, lively atmosphere makes it a great spot for sharing small plates with friends.

Café Charbon

Café Charbon is a historic café located on Rue Oberkampf, known for its classic Parisian vibe and lively ambiance. It serves a mix of traditional French dishes and contemporary favorites, making it a popular spot for both locals and tourists. The vintage decor and bustling energy make it a perfect place for a meal or a drink.

Bistrot Paul Bert

Bistrot Paul Bert is a classic Parisian bistro celebrated for its traditional French cuisine and nostalgic charm. The menu features expertly prepared dishes like steak frites, duck breast, and crème brûlée. The bistro's timeless decor and warm service have made it a beloved institution in the arrondissement.

Summary

The 11th Arrondissement (Popincourt) of Paris is a dynamic and culturally rich district, known for its historical significance, vibrant nightlife, and diverse culinary scene. From the historically pivotal Place de la Bastille and the iconic Cirque d'Hiver to the lively Rue Oberkampf and the artisanal Faubourg Saint-Antoine, the arrondissement offers a wide array of experiences.

Visitors can explore the district's rich history through its landmarks, enjoy performances in historic venues, and immerse themselves in the local culture through its bustling streets and markets. The area is also renowned for its gastronomic offerings, with a variety of acclaimed restaurants and bistros that showcase both traditional and innovative French cuisine.

Whether you're looking to delve into Parisian history, enjoy the vibrant nightlife, or savor exceptional food, the 11th Arrondissement provides a multifaceted and authentic Parisian experience that reflects the city's past and present.

12TH ARRONDISSEMENT (REUILLY)

Main Interesting History Facts of the 12th Arrondissement

The 12th Arrondissement, also known as Reuilly, is a diverse and historically rich district in Paris. It is known for its expansive green spaces, dynamic cultural institutions, and significant historical landmarks.

Place de la Nation

Place de la Nation is a major square in the 12th Arrondissement, named in honor of the French Nation. It played a significant role during the French Revolution, serving as a site for public executions. Today, it features the monumental statue "Le Triomphe de la République," symbolizing liberty and the republic.

Viaduc des Arts

The Viaduc des Arts is a unique architectural feature of the 12th Arrondissement. Originally a railway viaduct built in 1859, it was transformed in the 1990s into a hub for artisans and craftspeople. The arches now house various workshops, galleries, and boutiques, while the elevated Promenade Plantée (Coulée verte René-Dumont) above it offers a scenic green walkway.

Gare de Lyon

Gare de Lyon, one of the six main railway stations in Paris, opened in 1900 for the Exposition Universelle. It is known for its iconic clock tower and the elegant Train Bleu restaurant. The station connects Paris with destinations in the south of France and beyond, making it a vital transportation hub.

Bercy

The Bercy area, formerly known for its wine warehouses, has undergone significant redevelopment. It is now home to Bercy Village, a charming shopping and dining area, and the AccorHotels Arena, a major concert and sports venue. The Parc de Bercy, with its beautiful gardens and cultural facilities, is also a highlight of the area.

Palais de la Porte Dorée

Built for the Colonial Exhibition of 1931, the Palais de la Porte Dorée is an Art Deco masterpiece. It currently houses the Musée de l'Histoire de l'Immigration, which explores the history of immigration in France, and an aquarium. The building's stunning facade and interior murals make it a significant cultural landmark.

Things To Do You Can't Miss

The 12th Arrondissement offers a range of activities and attractions that highlight its historical significance, cultural diversity, and natural beauty.

Stroll Along the Promenade Plantée

Walk along the Promenade Plantée (Coulée verte René-Dumont), an elevated park built on a former railway line. The scenic walkway stretches from Bastille to the Bois de Vincennes, offering beautiful views, lush gardens, and a peaceful escape from the city's hustle and bustle.

Explore Parc de Bercy

Visit Parc de Bercy, a large park with varied landscapes, including formal gardens, lawns, and ponds. The park also features cultural attractions like the Cinémathèque Française, dedicated to the history of cinema, and Bercy Village, a charming area with shops, restaurants, and a lively atmosphere.

Discover the Viaduc des Arts

Explore the Viaduc des Arts, where you can browse the workshops, galleries, and boutiques housed in the viaduct's arches. This unique space showcases the work of artisans and craftspeople, offering a fascinating glimpse into contemporary Parisian creativity.

Visit Gare de Lyon

Admire the architectural beauty of Gare de Lyon and enjoy a meal at the historic Train Bleu restaurant. The station's impressive facade, iconic clock tower, and elegant interior make it a must-see landmark.

Experience the Palais de la Porte Dorée

Tour the Palais de la Porte Dorée to appreciate its Art Deco architecture and visit the Musée de l'Histoire de l'Immigration. The museum's exhibitions provide insightful perspectives on France's diverse cultural history, while the aquarium offers a captivating underwater experience.

Enjoy a Concert or Event at AccorHotels Arena

Attend a concert or sports event at the AccorHotels Arena, one of Paris's premier entertainment venues. The arena hosts a wide range of events, from international music acts to major sporting competitions, ensuring a lively and exciting atmosphere.

Relax in Bois de Vincennes

Spend time in Bois de Vincennes, Paris's largest public park, which offers a variety of recreational activities. Explore its lakes, botanical garden, and the Parc Floral de Paris, or visit the Château de Vincennes, a historic medieval fortress.

What to Eat and Famous Restaurants

The 12th Arrondissement boasts a diverse culinary scene, with options ranging from traditional French cuisine to innovative international dishes.

Le Train Bleu

Le Train Bleu, located in Gare de Lyon, is a historic restaurant offering a luxurious dining experience. The menu features classic French cuisine, including dishes like foie gras, roast lamb, and crème brûlée. The opulent decor, with its frescoes and chandeliers, transports diners to a bygone era.

L'Ébauchoir

L'Ébauchoir is a beloved bistro known for its warm ambiance and hearty French fare. The menu includes traditional dishes like duck confit, steak tartare, and seasonal vegetables, all prepared with fresh, local ingredients. The cozy setting and friendly service make it a favorite among locals and visitors.

Bistrot Paul Bert

Bistrot Paul Bert is a classic Parisian bistro renowned for its traditional French dishes and retro charm. The menu features expertly prepared dishes like steak frites, sole meunière, and delicious desserts such as tarte Tatin. The bistro's nostalgic ambiance and consistently high-quality food have made it a beloved institution in the area.

Le Square Trousseau

Le Square Trousseau is another gem offering a quintessential French dining experience. Located near the Marché d'Aligre, this bistro is known for its elegant decor, including vintage mirrors and tiled floors, and its menu of Parisian classics like onion soup, roast chicken, and profiteroles. The terrace offers a lovely spot for people-watching.

Blue Valentine

Blue Valentine is a modern bistro with an inventive menu that blends traditional French techniques with contemporary flavors. The seasonal menu changes regularly, but you can expect dishes like octopus with black garlic, guinea fowl with truffle jus, and creative desserts. The sleek, intimate setting and attentive service make it perfect for a special night out.

East Mamma

East Mamma is part of the Big Mamma group, known for bringing authentic Italian cuisine to Paris. The menu features homemade pasta, Neapolitan-style pizza, and delicious antipasti, all made with ingredients sourced directly from Italy. The vibrant, rustic atmosphere and friendly vibe attract a lively crowd.

Summary

The 12th Arrondissement (Reuilly) of Paris is a dynamic and diverse district, offering a rich tapestry of history, culture, and green spaces. From the historic Place de la Nation and the architectural marvel of Gare de Lyon to the tranquil Promenade Plantée and the expansive Bois de Vincennes, the arrondissement is full of attractions that cater to various interests.

Visitors can explore its historical landmarks, enjoy its cultural institutions like the Palais de la Porte Dorée, and relax in its beautiful parks. The area is also a food lover's paradise, with a variety of renowned restaurants and bistros offering both traditional French cuisine and international flavors.

Whether you're interested in history, culture, nature, or gastronomy, the 12th Arrondissement provides a multifaceted and enriching Parisian experience that reflects the city's vibrant and diverse character.

13TH ARRONDISSEMENT (GOBELINS)

Main Interesting History Facts of the 13th Arrondissement

The 13th Arrondissement, also known as Gobelins, is a dynamic and eclectic district in Paris, rich in history and cultural diversity. It is renowned for its industrial past, modern architectural developments, and vibrant multicultural communities.

Manufacture des Gobelins

The Manufacture des Gobelins is a historic tapestry factory founded in the 17th century by Louis XIV. It has produced exquisite tapestries and upholstery for French royalty and government buildings for centuries. The factory is still operational and offers guided tours, showcasing its significant contribution to French art and craftsmanship.

Quartier de la Butte-aux-Cailles

The Quartier de la Butte-aux-Cailles is a charming, village-like neighborhood known for its narrow, cobblestone streets and distinctive architecture. Historically, it was a working-class area with mills and factories. Today, it is famous for its vibrant street art, lively nightlife, and unique character, retaining a sense of old-world charm amidst modern developments.

Bibliothèque Nationale de France (BNF)

The Bibliothèque Nationale de France (National Library of France), located in the 13th Arrondissement, is one of the most significant cultural institutions in Paris. The François-Mitterrand site, inaugurated in 1996, features four towering glass buildings arranged around a central garden. The library houses millions of books, manuscripts, and historical documents, making it a vital resource for researchers and scholars.

Paris Rive Gauche

Paris Rive Gauche is a large urban development project that has transformed former industrial areas into modern residential, commercial, and cultural spaces. The district includes innovative architectural designs, green spaces, and vibrant public areas, reflecting the arrondissement's dynamic evolution and commitment to sustainable urban living.

Things To Do You Can't Miss

The 13th Arrondissement offers a variety of activities that highlight its historical significance, cultural diversity, and modern developments.

Visit the Manufacture des Gobelins

Explore the Manufacture des Gobelins to learn about the history and artistry of French tapestry making. Guided tours provide insights into the traditional techniques and the factory's role in French cultural heritage.

Wander Through Quartier de la Butte-aux-Cailles

Stroll through the Quartier de la Butte-aux-Cailles to enjoy its unique atmosphere, vibrant street art, and charming cafés. The neighborhood's blend of historic charm and contemporary creativity makes it a delightful area to explore.

Discover the Bibliothèque Nationale de France

Visit the Bibliothèque Nationale de France to explore its vast collection of books and manuscripts, attend exhibitions, or simply admire the modern architectural design of the François-Mitterrand site. The library's central garden provides a tranquil escape in the midst of the bustling city.

Explore Paris Rive Gauche

Take a walk through the Paris Rive Gauche district to see its modern architectural developments and green spaces. The area is home to various cultural institutions, shops, and restaurants, offering a glimpse into the future of urban living in Paris.

Admire the Street Art

The 13th Arrondissement is renowned for its impressive street art. Take a self-guided tour to see large-scale murals and graffiti by renowned artists like Invader, Shepard Fairey, and C215. The district's commitment to public art has turned it into an open-air gallery.

Visit Chinatown

The 13th Arrondissement is home to Paris's largest Chinatown. Explore the vibrant streets filled with Asian supermarkets, restaurants, and shops. Enjoy authentic Asian cuisine, particularly during the Chinese New Year celebrations, which feature colorful parades and cultural performances.

What to Eat and Famous Restaurants

The 13th Arrondissement offers a diverse culinary scene, reflecting its multicultural population and innovative spirit.

La Tour d'Argent

La Tour d'Argent is a legendary restaurant offering a luxurious dining experience with stunning views of the Seine and Notre-Dame Cathedral. Established in 1582, it is known for its classic French cuisine, including dishes like pressed duck and foie gras. The elegant setting and exceptional service make it a must-visit for gourmet enthusiasts.

Le Virtus

Le Virtus is a modern French restaurant that focuses on seasonal ingredients and creative presentations. The menu features inventive dishes that highlight the chef's culinary expertise and the use of fresh, local produce. The minimalist decor and refined atmosphere provide the perfect backdrop for a memorable dining experience.

Lao Douang Chan

Lao Douang Chan is a popular spot in Chinatown, offering authentic Laotian and Thai cuisine. The menu includes flavorful dishes like larb (spicy minced meat salad), pad thai, and various curries. The casual setting and friendly service make it a great place to enjoy a delicious and affordable meal.

Chez Gladines

Chez Gladines is a lively Basque restaurant known for its hearty portions and convivial atmosphere. The menu features traditional dishes like duck confit, Basque chicken, and hearty salads. The rustic decor and bustling environment make it a favorite among locals and visitors alike.

Pho 14

Pho 14 is a beloved Vietnamese restaurant located in the heart of Paris's Chinatown. It is famous for its authentic and flavorful pho, a traditional Vietnamese noodle soup. The menu also includes other Vietnamese favorites like spring rolls, banh mi, and vermicelli bowls. The casual ambiance and affordable prices make it a popular choice for a quick and satisfying meal.

L'Auberge Etchegorry

L'Auberge Etchegorry is a charming Basque restaurant that has been serving traditional Basque cuisine since 1953. The menu features specialties like axoa (a veal stew), piperade (a Basque vegetable dish), and various seafood dishes. The cozy, rustic decor and warm hospitality make it a great spot for experiencing Basque culture and cuisine.

Summary

The 13th Arrondissement (Gobelins) of Paris is a vibrant and diverse district that seamlessly blends its rich historical heritage with modern developments. From the historic Manufacture des Gobelins and the charming Quartier de la Butte-aux-Cailles to the contemporary Paris Rive Gauche and the impressive Bibliothèque Nationale de France, the arrondissement offers a wide array of attractions and activities.

Visitors can explore its historical sites, enjoy its cultural institutions, and experience its lively street art scene. The area is also home to Paris's largest Chinatown, offering a unique cultural experience and a diverse culinary scene with everything from classic French cuisine to authentic Asian dishes.

Whether you're interested in history, culture, modern architecture, or gastronomy, the 13th Arrondissement provides a multifaceted and enriching Parisian experience that reflects the city's dynamic and ever-evolving character.

14TH ARRONDISSEMENT (OBSERVATOIRE)

Main Interesting History Facts of the 14th Arrondissement

The 14th Arrondissement of Paris, also known as Observatoire, is a district rich in history, culture, and architectural landmarks. It is known for its bohemian past, scientific contributions, and vibrant communities.

Paris Observatory

The Paris Observatory (Observatoire de Paris) is one of the oldest astronomical observatories in the world, founded in 1667. It played a crucial role in the development of modern astronomy and remains an active research institution. The observatory's historic buildings and scientific instruments are a testament to its long-standing contribution to astronomy.

Montparnasse

Montparnasse is a historic neighborhood in the 14th Arrondissement that became a hub for artists, writers, and intellectuals during the early 20th century. Famous figures such as Pablo Picasso, Ernest Hemingway, and Jean-Paul Sartre frequented its cafés and studios. The area is also home to the Montparnasse Cemetery, where many notable figures are buried.

Catacombs of Paris

The Catacombs of Paris are an extensive network of underground ossuaries that hold the remains of over six million people. Established in the late 18th century to address the city's overcrowded cemeteries, the catacombs offer a unique and eerie glimpse into Paris's history. Visitors can tour a small portion of this vast subterranean labyrinth.

Fondation Cartier pour l'Art Contemporain

The Fondation Cartier pour l'Art Contemporain is a contemporary art museum located in the 14th Arrondissement. Founded in 1984 by the Cartier jewelry company, the museum showcases cutting-edge contemporary art in a stunning glass building designed by architect Jean Nouvel. It has become a major cultural institution in Paris.

Things To Do You Can't Miss

The 14th Arrondissement offers a variety of activities and attractions that highlight its historical significance and vibrant cultural scene.

Visit the Paris Observatory

Explore the Paris Observatory to learn about its historical significance and ongoing scientific research. While access to the observatory is limited, special events and guided tours occasionally provide opportunities to visit this historic site and its impressive collection of astronomical instruments.

Explore the Catacombs of Paris

Take a tour of the Catacombs of Paris for a unique and fascinating experience. The tour guides visitors through a small section of the underground tunnels, where they can see the carefully arranged bones and learn about the history of this macabre attraction.

Stroll Through Montparnasse

Wander the streets of Montparnasse to soak in its artistic and literary heritage. Visit the famous cafés like La Coupole, Le Dôme, and La Rotonde, where many famous artists and writers once gathered. You can also explore the Montparnasse Cemetery to see the graves of notable figures such as Jean-Paul Sartre, Simone de Beauvoir, and Samuel Beckett.

Enjoy Contemporary Art at Fondation Cartier

Visit the Fondation Cartier pour l'Art Contemporain to experience innovative contemporary art exhibitions. The museum's striking architecture and lush garden provide a serene backdrop for its diverse range of artworks, installations, and performances.

Discover Parc Montsouris

Parc Montsouris is a beautiful English-style park in the 14th Arrondissement, perfect for a leisurely stroll or a picnic. The park features expansive lawns, winding paths, a lake, and a variety of trees and flowers. It's a peaceful oasis in the bustling city and a favorite spot for locals.

What to Eat and Famous Restaurants

The 14th Arrondissement offers a diverse culinary scene, with a range of options from traditional French cuisine to international flavors.

La Coupole

La Coupole is a legendary brasserie in Montparnasse, known for its Art Deco interior and rich history. The menu features classic French dishes such as oysters, seafood platters, and steak frites. The vibrant atmosphere and historic charm make it a must-visit.

Le Dôme

Le Dôme is another historic brasserie in Montparnasse, famous for its seafood. The restaurant has been a favorite among artists and intellectuals for over a century. The elegant setting and high-quality seafood dishes, including lobster and sole meunière, make it a top dining destination.

La Rotonde

La Rotonde is a renowned café and brasserie that has been a gathering place for artists and writers since the early 20th century. The menu offers a range of French classics, including escargots, duck confit, and crème brûlée. The historic ambiance and excellent cuisine make it a delightful dining experience.

Le Severo

Le Severo is a popular bistro known for its focus on high-quality meat. The menu features expertly cooked steaks, including côte de boeuf and entrecôte, served with delicious sides like pommes frites and seasonal vegetables. The intimate setting and attentive service make it a great spot for meat lovers.

L'Assiette

L'Assiette is a charming bistro offering traditional French cuisine with a modern twist. The menu, crafted by chef David Rathgeber, features dishes like cassoulet, foie gras, and duck breast, all prepared with fresh, seasonal ingredients. The cozy, rustic ambiance and innovative yet comforting food make it a standout in the 14th Arrondissement.

Crêperie Josselin

Crêperie Josselin is a beloved spot for enjoying traditional Breton crêpes and galettes. The menu includes a wide variety of savory and sweet options, such as the classic ham and cheese galette or the indulgent caramel and apple crêpe. The charming, rustic interior and delicious crêpes make it a favorite among locals and tourists.

Summary

The 14th Arrondissement (Observatoire) of Paris is a district that embodies the city's rich historical legacy and vibrant cultural life. From the scientific advancements of the Paris Observatory and the artistic heritage of Montparnasse to the eerie allure of the Catacombs and the contemporary flair of the Fondation Cartier, the arrondissement offers a wide array of attractions that cater to diverse interests.

Visitors can immerse themselves in the district's historical and scientific significance, enjoy its lush parks, and explore its dynamic art scene. The culinary landscape of the 14th Arrondissement is equally impressive, featuring a mix of historic brasseries, contemporary bistros, and international flavors.

Whether you're a history buff, an art enthusiast, a foodie, or simply looking to experience a lesser-known yet fascinating part of Paris, the 14th Arrondissement provides a multifaceted and enriching experience that highlights the city's unique blend of tradition and modernity.

15TH ARRONDISSEMENT (VAUGIRARD)

Main Interesting History Facts of the 15th Arrondissement

The 15th Arrondissement, also known as Vaugirard, is the largest district in Paris both in terms of area and population. It offers a mix of residential neighborhoods, historical landmarks, and modern attractions.

Village Vaugirard

Before becoming part of Paris in 1860, the area was a separate village known as Vaugirard. The village's agricultural roots can still be felt in some of its quieter streets and local markets, giving parts of the arrondissement a small-town charm amidst the bustling city.

Eiffel Tower's Backyard

While the Eiffel Tower itself is located in the 7th Arrondissement, its presence has significantly influenced the 15th Arrondissement. The area around the tower, particularly the Champ de Mars park, is a major draw for both tourists and locals looking for scenic views and leisure activities.

Montparnasse Tower

The Montparnasse Tower (Tour Montparnasse) is one of the most notable modern landmarks in Paris and offers stunning panoramic views of the city. Completed in 1973, it stands as a symbol of modern architectural ambition and has a viewing platform that provides one of the best vantage points to see the Eiffel Tower.

Parc André Citroën

This contemporary park, located on the former site of the Citroën car manufacturing plant, is an example of urban renewal. Opened in 1992, it features modern landscaping, themed gardens, and even a tethered helium balloon that offers rides for a unique aerial perspective of Paris.

Things To Do You Can't Miss

The 15th Arrondissement offers a variety of activities that cater to different interests, from historical landmarks to modern attractions.

Explore Parc André Citroën

Visit Parc André Citroën to enjoy its modern design and beautiful themed gardens. Take a ride on the Ballon de Paris, a tethered helium balloon, for an unforgettable aerial view of the city and the Seine River.

Visit the Montparnasse Tower

Ascend the Montparnasse Tower to its 56th-floor observation deck for a breathtaking panoramic view of Paris. The tower's height provides an excellent vantage point to capture the city's skyline, including a unique perspective of the Eiffel Tower.

Discover the Village Vaugirard

Wander through the quieter streets of the former village of Vaugirard. Explore local markets, quaint shops, and charming cafés that offer a glimpse into the area's pastoral past amid its urban setting.

Tour the Musée Bourdelle

The Musée Bourdelle is dedicated to the works of sculptor Antoine Bourdelle, a student of Auguste Rodin. The museum includes Bourdelle's former studio and garden, displaying a vast collection of his sculptures, drawings, and personal artifacts. It's a hidden gem for art lovers.

Relax at Parc Georges-Brassens

Parc Georges-Brassens is a picturesque park named after the famous French singer-songwriter. The park features a vineyard, a rose garden, and a literary market held on weekends. It's a perfect spot for a relaxing stroll or a picnic.

Experience Aquaboulevard

Aquaboulevard is the largest urban water park in Europe, offering a variety of pools, slides, and water activities. It's a fun destination for families and anyone looking to enjoy a day of aquatic adventure.

What to Eat and Famous Restaurants

The 15th Arrondissement has a diverse culinary scene, with options ranging from traditional French cuisine to international flavors.

La Cantine du Troquet

La Cantine du Troquet is a popular bistro offering Basque-inspired cuisine. The menu features hearty dishes such as duck confit, lamb shoulder, and flavorful seafood. The warm and lively atmosphere makes it a favorite among locals and visitors alike.

Le Ciel de Paris

Located on the 56th floor of the Montparnasse Tower, Le Ciel de Paris offers fine dining with a spectacular view. The menu includes contemporary French cuisine, and the panoramic views of Paris provide a stunning backdrop for a memorable dining experience.

L'Os à Moelle

L'Os à Moelle is a renowned bistro known for its focus on traditional French fare using high-quality ingredients. The menu changes regularly to reflect seasonal produce, and the cozy, intimate setting enhances the dining experience.

Bistro du Dôme

Bistro du Dôme is a charming eatery that offers a seafood-focused menu, including fresh oysters, lobster, and fish dishes. The restaurant prides itself on its high-quality seafood and elegant yet relaxed ambiance.

Le Quinzième

Le Quinzième is a Michelin-starred restaurant by chef Cyril Lignac, known for its inventive French cuisine. The menu features dishes that blend traditional techniques with modern flavors, all presented with artistic flair. The sophisticated setting and exceptional service make it a top dining destination.

Summary

The 15th Arrondissement (Vaugirard) of Paris is a diverse and dynamic district that combines residential neighborhoods with historical landmarks and modern attractions. From the quiet charm of Village Vaugirard to the panoramic views from the Montparnasse Tower, the arrondissement offers a rich tapestry of experiences.

16TH ARRONDISSEMENT (PASSY)

Main Interesting History Facts of the 16th Arrondissement

The 16th Arrondissement, also known as Passy, is one of the most affluent and prestigious districts in Paris. It is known for its elegant architecture, green spaces, and cultural landmarks.

Historical Significance

The area of Passy has a rich history that dates back to the Roman era. It became a fashionable suburb in the 19th century, attracting wealthy Parisians who built luxurious mansions and gardens. The arrondissement was officially incorporated into Paris in 1860.

Architectural Landmarks

The 16th Arrondissement is renowned for its stunning examples of Haussmannian and Art Nouveau architecture. It is home to numerous private mansions, embassies, and the iconic Maison de la Radio, an impressive circular building that serves as the headquarters for Radio France.

The Birthplace of Cinema

The arrondissement is historically significant for being the site of the first public screening of a motion picture. The Lumière brothers showcased their invention, the cinematograph, at the Salon Indien du Grand Café in 1895, marking the birth of cinema.

The Trocadéro

The Trocadéro area, with its grand esplanade and fountains, offers one of the best views of the Eiffel Tower. The Palais de Chaillot, built for the 1937 World's Fair, houses several museums, including the Musée de l'Homme and the Cité de l'Architecture et du Patrimoine.

Things To Do You Can't Miss

Visit the Trocadéro

The Trocadéro is a must-see for its breathtaking views of the Eiffel Tower. The expansive esplanade and its gardens are perfect for a leisurely stroll, and the Palais de Chaillot's museums offer fascinating exhibitions on architecture, maritime history, and anthropology.

Explore the Bois de Boulogne

The Bois de Boulogne is one of Paris's largest parks, offering vast green spaces, lakes, and wooded areas for outdoor activities. You can rent a boat, visit the Jardin d'Acclimatation amusement park, or explore the Fondation Louis Vuitton, a contemporary art museum designed by Frank Gehry.

Discover the Musée Marmottan Monet

This museum houses the world's largest collection of works by Claude Monet, including the famous painting "Impression, Sunrise." The Musée Marmottan Monet also features works by other Impressionist and Post-Impressionist artists, making it a treasure trove for art lovers.

Relax in the Parc de Bagatelle

Located within the Bois de Boulogne, the Parc de Bagatelle is a beautiful English-style garden known for its rose garden, water lilies, and charming follies. It's an ideal spot for a peaceful walk or a romantic picnic.

Tour the Palais de Tokyo

The Palais de Tokyo is one of the largest centers for contemporary art in Europe. It hosts cutting-edge exhibitions, performances, and installations, making it a dynamic space for art enthusiasts to explore.

Visit the Maison de Balzac

The Maison de Balzac is a small museum dedicated to the life and works of the famous French writer Honoré de Balzac. The museum is located in the house where Balzac lived and wrote some of his most important works. It provides a fascinating insight into his life and the literary scene of the 19th century.

What to Eat and Famous Restaurants

The 16th Arrondissement offers a variety of dining options, from Michelin-starred restaurants to charming bistros and cafés.

Le Relais de l'Entrecôte

This renowned restaurant is famous for its simple yet delicious menu: a walnut salad followed by steak frites with a secret sauce. The no-reservation policy often results in long lines, but the meal is well worth the wait.

La Grande Cascade

Located in the Bois de Boulogne, La Grande Cascade offers a luxurious dining experience in a historical setting. The Michelin-starred restaurant serves gourmet French cuisine in an elegant Belle Époque pavilion.

Astrance

Astrance is a Michelin-starred restaurant known for its innovative and refined French cuisine. Chef Pascal Barbot creates unique tasting menus that delight the senses. Reservations are essential due to its popularity and limited seating.

Le Stella

Le Stella is a classic Parisian brasserie that has been serving traditional French dishes since 1956. The menu includes favorites such as escargots, steak tartare, and sole meunière, all prepared with high-quality ingredients.

Aux Trois Nagas

For a taste of Thai cuisine, Aux Trois Nagas offers an authentic experience with dishes like pad Thai, green curry, and mango sticky rice. The restaurant is known for its flavorful dishes and warm ambiance.

Carette

Located near the Trocadéro, Carette is a famous pâtisserie and tearoom offering delicious pastries, macarons, and light meals. It's a perfect spot for a leisurely breakfast or an afternoon tea with a view of the Eiffel Tower.

Summary

The 16th Arrondissement (Passy) of Paris is a district that combines historical significance, architectural beauty, cultural richness, and natural splendor. From its role in the birth of cinema to its stunning views of the Eiffel Tower from the Trocadéro, the arrondissement offers a wealth of experiences.

17TH ARRONDISSEMENT (BATIGNOLLES-MONCEAU)

Main Interesting History Facts of the 17th Arrondissement

The 17th Arrondissement, also known as Batignolles-Monceau, is a diverse and vibrant district in Paris that combines historical charm, elegant architecture, and a lively cultural scene.

Historical Background

Originally a collection of villages, the area was incorporated into Paris in 1860. The neighborhood of Batignolles, in particular, has a rich history as a hub for artists and intellectuals in the 19th century. Famous figures like Édouard Manet and the poet Paul Verlaine were associated with this area.

Architectural Landmarks

The arrondissement is known for its eclectic architecture, ranging from Haussmannian buildings to modern developments. The Parc Monceau, created in the 18th century, is a notable example of English-style gardens in Paris and is surrounded by grand townhouses.

The Batignolles Group

In the late 19th century, the Batignolles neighborhood became famous for a group of avant-garde artists who gathered there, known as the Batignolles Group. This group included painters like Édouard Manet and Edgar Degas, who were precursors to the Impressionist movement.

Modern Development

The northwestern part of the arrondissement has seen significant modern development, particularly with the construction of the new Cité Judiciaire and the Parc Clichy-Batignolles – Martin Luther King, which has transformed the area into a dynamic urban space.

Things To Do You Can't Miss

Stroll Through Parc Monceau

Parc Monceau is a beautifully landscaped English-style park with winding paths, statues, and a variety of trees and plants. It's perfect for a leisurely stroll, a jog, or a picnic. The park also features a charming collection of follies, including a miniature Egyptian pyramid and a Corinthian colonnade.

Explore the Batignolles Neighborhood

Wander through the Batignolles neighborhood to experience its bohemian charm. Visit the Place de Clichy, a bustling square, and enjoy a coffee at one of the many cafés. Don't miss the Marché des Batignolles, an organic market offering fresh produce and local delicacies.

Visit the Musée Nissim de Camondo

This museum is housed in a beautifully preserved mansion near Parc Monceau. It showcases an exquisite collection of 18th-century French furniture, art, and decorative objects, providing a glimpse into the luxury and elegance of the period.

Discover the Epinettes and Ternes Quarters

The Epinettes and Ternes areas offer a mix of traditional and contemporary Parisian life. The Rue de Lévis market street in the Ternes quarter is a great place to shop for fresh produce, cheese, and other gourmet items.

Enjoy the Parc Clichy-Batignolles – Martin Luther King

This modern park is a green oasis with contemporary landscaping, playgrounds, and sports facilities. It's a great place for families and anyone looking to relax in a more modern urban park setting.

Experience the Cité Judiciaire

The new Cité Judiciaire is an impressive modern complex housing Paris's judicial courts. Designed by architect Renzo Piano, it's a striking example of contemporary architecture and urban planning.

What to Eat and Famous Restaurants

The 17th Arrondissement offers a variety of dining options, from traditional French bistros to contemporary eateries.

Les Poulettes Batignolles

This cozy bistro offers a warm atmosphere and a menu featuring classic French dishes with a modern twist. The focus is on fresh, seasonal ingredients, and the wine list is carefully curated.

Coretta

Located near the Parc Clichy-Batignolles – Martin Luther King, Coretta is a contemporary restaurant offering inventive cuisine in a sleek, modern setting. The dishes are beautifully presented and the flavors are bold and creative.

Le P'tit Canon

A charming neighborhood bistro, Le P'tit Canon is known for its friendly service and delicious traditional French cuisine. The menu includes favorites like duck confit, steak frites, and crème brûlée.

La Table de l'Elysée

This elegant restaurant offers refined French dining with a focus on high-quality ingredients and expert preparation. The ambiance is sophisticated, making it perfect for a special occasion.

Le Bistrot des Dames

Located near the Place de Clichy, this bistro has a lovely garden terrace that's perfect for a relaxed meal. The menu features a mix of French and Mediterranean dishes, and the atmosphere is laid-back and welcoming.

Les Fils à Maman

For a nostalgic dining experience, head to Les Fils à Maman, where the menu is inspired by childhood favorites and comfort food. The quirky decor and playful dishes make it a fun and unique dining spot.

Summary

The 17th Arrondissement (Batignolles-Monceau) is a dynamic and diverse district that offers a blend of historical charm, architectural beauty, and contemporary vibrancy. From the artistic heritage of the Batignolles neighborhood to the elegant Parc Monceau and modern developments like the Parc Clichy-Batignolles – Martin Luther King, there's something for everyone in this lively part of Paris.

18TH ARRONDISSEMENT (BUTTE-MONTMARTRE)

Main Interesting History Facts of the 18th Arrondissement

The 18th Arrondissement, also known as Butte-Montmartre, is one of Paris's most iconic and picturesque districts. It is famous for its bohemian history, artistic heritage, and stunning views of the city.

Historical Background

Montmartre was originally a village outside Paris, annexed to the city in 1860. It became a hub for artists and intellectuals in the late 19th and early 20th centuries. The area is known for its steep, narrow streets, charming squares, and historic buildings.

Artistic Heritage

Montmartre was home to many famous artists, including Pablo Picasso, Vincent van Gogh, and Henri de Toulouse-Lautrec. The neighborhood's vibrant artistic scene made it a center of the avant-garde movement. The Bateau-Lavoir, a building in Montmartre, housed many of these artists in their early careers.

The Moulin Rouge

Opened in 1889, the Moulin Rouge is one of the most famous cabarets in the world. Known for its extravagant performances and the birthplace of the can-can dance, it played a significant role in the nightlife and culture of Paris.

The Basilica of Sacré-Cœur

The Basilica of Sacré-Cœur, completed in 1914, is one of Montmartre's most recognizable landmarks. Located at the summit of the Butte Montmartre, it offers panoramic views of Paris. The basilica's white domes and Roman-Byzantine architecture make it a striking feature of the Parisian skyline.

Things To Do You Can't Miss

Visit the Basilica of Sacré-Cœur

Climb to the top of the Butte Montmartre to visit the Basilica of Sacré-Cœur. Enjoy the stunning architecture and take in the breathtaking views of Paris from the church's steps or dome.

Explore Place du Tertre

This lively square is filled with artists displaying their work and painting portraits. It retains the bohemian spirit of Montmartre and is a great place to soak in the artistic atmosphere.

Wander Through the Montmartre Museum

Located in a historic house where several artists lived, the Montmartre Museum showcases the history of the neighborhood, its artistic heritage, and the lives of the artists who made Montmartre famous.

Discover the Wall of Love

Located in the Jehan Rictus Square, the Wall of Love (Le Mur des Je t'aime) is an art installation featuring the words "I love you" written in over 250 languages. It's a romantic spot for couples and a unique piece of street art.

Visit the Moulin Rouge

Experience a show at the Moulin Rouge to see the famous can-can dance and elaborate performances. The cabaret's history and vibrant shows make it a must-visit attraction in Montmartre.

Explore the Montmartre Vineyards

One of the last remaining vineyards in Paris, the Clos Montmartre, is located on the northern slope of the hill. The vineyard produces a small amount of wine each year and adds to the neighborhood's unique charm.

What to Eat and Famous Restaurants

Montmartre offers a variety of dining options, from traditional French bistros to trendy cafés.

Le Moulin de la Galette

This historic restaurant, housed in a former windmill, offers classic French cuisine in a charming setting. It's known for its delicious dishes and historical significance.

La Mascotte

A traditional brasserie in the heart of Montmartre, La Mascotte serves classic French dishes, including seafood platters and steak frites. The lively atmosphere and authentic cuisine make it a popular choice.

Café des Deux Moulins

Famous for its appearance in the film "Amélie," this café offers a cozy ambiance and a menu of French classics. It's a great spot for a coffee or a meal while soaking in the cinematic history.

Le Relais Gascon

Known for its hearty portions and rustic cuisine, Le Relais Gascon offers traditional dishes from the southwest of France. The salads, topped with generous servings of meats and cheeses, are particularly popular.

Sacré Fleur

Located near the Sacré-Cœur, this restaurant specializes in grilled meats and offers a warm, intimate dining experience. The menu features a variety of meat dishes, including steak, lamb, and duck.

Le Refuge des Fondus

For a fun and unique dining experience, head to Le Refuge des Fondus. This quirky restaurant serves fondue and wine in baby bottles, creating a playful and memorable atmosphere.

Summary

The 18th Arrondissement (Butte-Montmartre) is a district rich in history, culture, and artistic legacy. From the iconic Basilica of Sacré-Cœur and the lively Place du Tertre to the historic cabarets and charming streets, Montmartre offers a unique and enchanting Parisian experience. The area's diverse dining options, vibrant arts scene, and breathtaking views make it a must-visit destination for anyone exploring Paris.

19TH ARRONDISSEMENT (BUTTES-CHAUMONT)

Main Interesting History Facts of the 19th Arrondissement

The 19th Arrondissement, also known as Buttes-Chaumont, is one of Paris's most diverse and vibrant districts. It is known for its expansive parks, cultural venues, and dynamic neighborhoods.

Historical Background

The 19th Arrondissement was incorporated into Paris in 1860. Historically, it was an industrial area with factories and warehouses. Over time, it has transformed into a residential and cultural hub, with significant urban renewal projects reshaping the landscape.

Parc des Buttes-Chaumont

Created in 1867 by Napoleon III, Parc des Buttes-Chaumont is one of the largest green spaces in Paris. The park was constructed on the site of former quarries and features steep cliffs, a suspension bridge designed by Gustave Eiffel, and a Roman-style temple perched on a rocky island.

Canal de l'Ourcq and Canal Saint-Martin

These canals were originally built for transporting goods to and from Paris. Today, they are popular leisure spots, with scenic walkways, boat rides, and trendy cafés lining their banks. The canals play a key role in the arrondissement's recreational life.

La Villette

Originally an industrial area, La Villette has been transformed into a major cultural and recreational complex. The Parc de la Villette, one of the largest parks in Paris, includes attractions such as the Cité des Sciences et de l'Industrie (a science museum), the Philharmonie de Paris, and the Zénith concert hall.

Things To Do You Can't Miss

Explore Parc des Buttes-Chaumont

Enjoy a stroll or a picnic in this picturesque park. Visit the Temple de la Sibylle for panoramic views, walk across the suspension bridge, and explore the park's winding paths, waterfalls, and grottoes.

Visit the Cité des Sciences et de l'Industrie

This massive science museum is great for families and anyone interested in science and technology. It features interactive exhibits, a planetarium, and a submarine.

Stroll Along Canal de l'Ourcq and Canal Saint-Martin

Take a leisurely walk or bike ride along these scenic canals. Enjoy the vibrant atmosphere, street art, and the many bars and cafés that line the banks. You can also take a boat tour to see the canals from a different perspective.

Discover the Parc de la Villette

This modern park is a hub for cultural activities. Visit the Philharmonie de Paris for a concert, explore the themed gardens, or catch a film at the open-air cinema during the summer months.

Experience La Cité de la Musique

Part of the Parc de la Villette, La Cité de la Musique is a complex dedicated to music. It includes a music museum, concert halls, and a conservatory. The museum's collection of musical instruments is particularly impressive.

Enjoy the Zénith Paris

Attend a concert or event at the Zénith, one of Paris's largest concert halls. It hosts a wide range of performances, from rock concerts to comedy shows.

What to Eat and Famous Restaurants

The 19th Arrondissement offers a variety of dining options, from traditional French cuisine to international flavors.

Le Pavillon du Lac

Located within Parc des Buttes-Chaumont, this charming restaurant offers a beautiful setting with lake views. The menu features French and Mediterranean cuisine, perfect for a leisurely meal after exploring the park.

Le Baratin

A favorite among foodies, Le Baratin serves inventive French bistro fare. The menu changes frequently based on seasonal ingredients, and the wine list is excellent.

Rosa Bonheur

This guinguette-style bar and restaurant in Parc des Buttes-Chaumont is popular for its relaxed atmosphere and scenic location. Enjoy drinks and tapas on the outdoor terrace, especially during the warmer months.

Paname Brewing Company

Situated along the Canal de l'Ourcq, this brewpub offers a range of craft beers brewed on-site. The menu includes burgers, pizzas, and other pub fare. The outdoor seating area provides great views of the canal.

La Table de Botzaris

This cozy bistro near Parc des Buttes-Chaumont serves classic French dishes with a modern twist. The intimate setting and delicious food make it a great spot for a romantic dinner or a special occasion.

Summary

The 19th Arrondissement (Buttes-Chaumont) is a diverse and dynamic area that offers a mix of natural beauty, cultural attractions, and modern urban life. From the stunning Parc des Buttes-Chaumont to the vibrant Canal de l'Ourcq and the cultural hub of La Villette, there's something for everyone in this lively part of Paris. Whether you're interested in exploring parks, visiting museums, enjoying live music, or savoring delicious food, the 19th Arrondissement has plenty to offer.

20TH ARRONDISSEMENT (MÉNILMONTANT)

Main Interesting History Facts of the 20th Arrondissement

The 20th Arrondissement, also known as Ménilmontant, is one of Paris's most eclectic and culturally rich districts. It is renowned for its vibrant street art, diverse communities, and historic cemeteries.

Historical Background

The 20th Arrondissement was incorporated into Paris in 1860. Historically, it was a working-class neighborhood with a strong tradition of political activism. The area has a rich history of immigration, making it one of the most multicultural parts of the city.

Père Lachaise Cemetery

Opened in 1804, Père Lachaise is the largest cemetery in Paris and one of the most famous in the world. It is the final resting place of many notable figures, including Oscar Wilde, Jim Morrison, Edith Piaf, and Frédéric Chopin. The cemetery is also known for its beautiful monuments and serene atmosphere.

Belleville

Once a separate village, Belleville was annexed to Paris in 1860. It has a history of being a hub for artists and immigrants. The area is known for its bohemian vibe, ethnic diversity, and vibrant street life. Belleville was also the birthplace of famous French singer Edith Piaf.

Communard Wall (Mur des Fédérés)

Located in Père Lachaise Cemetery, the Communard Wall is a historical monument commemorating the 147 communards who were executed there following the fall of the Paris Commune in 1871. The wall is a significant symbol of the working-class struggles and revolutionary history of the area.

Things To Do You Can't Miss

Visit Père Lachaise Cemetery

Explore this iconic cemetery, known for its famous graves and beautiful monuments. Take a guided tour to learn about the history and notable figures buried here. It's a peaceful place for a reflective walk amidst the tombstones and sculptures.

Wander Through Belleville

Stroll through the vibrant streets of Belleville, known for its street art, ethnic eateries, and lively atmosphere. Visit the Belleville Market for fresh produce and local goods, and enjoy the panoramic views of Paris from Parc de Belleville.

Explore Parc de Belleville

This park offers some of the best views of Paris from its elevated terraces. It's a great place for a picnic or a leisurely walk. The park also features playgrounds, fountains, and beautiful landscaped gardens.

Discover the Street Art

The 20th Arrondissement is famous for its street art. Wander through the streets of Ménilmontant and Belleville to see murals, graffiti, and artistic installations. Rue Dénoyez is particularly well-known for its colorful street art.

Visit La Bellevilloise

This cultural venue hosts a variety of events, including concerts, art exhibitions, and film screenings. It's a great place to experience the local arts scene and enjoy live music in a historic setting.

Explore the Edith Piaf Museum

This small museum is dedicated to the life and legacy of Edith Piaf, one of France's most beloved singers. It's located in a private apartment and features memorabilia, photographs, and personal items related to Piaf's career.

What to Eat and Famous Restaurants

The 20th Arrondissement offers a diverse culinary scene, reflecting its multicultural population.

Le Baratin

This cozy bistro is a favorite among locals and food critics alike. It serves inventive French cuisine with a focus on fresh, seasonal ingredients. The wine list is also excellent.

La Vache Acrobate

A charming restaurant in the heart of Belleville, La Vache Acrobate offers a menu of French and Mediterranean dishes. The warm ambiance and delicious food make it a great spot for a casual meal.

Mama Shelter

Designed by Philippe Starck, Mama Shelter is a trendy hotel and restaurant offering a lively atmosphere and a menu of eclectic dishes. The rooftop terrace is a popular spot for drinks with a view.

Le Jourdain

Located near Père Lachaise Cemetery, Le Jourdain is known for its seafood dishes and relaxed vibe. The menu features fresh, high-quality ingredients and the wine selection is carefully curated.

Le Pure Café

A quintessential Parisian café, Le Pure Café offers a classic menu of French dishes and drinks. It's a great spot for a coffee or a casual meal while soaking in the local atmosphere.

Les Pâtes Vivantes

For a taste of authentic Chinese cuisine, head to Les Pâtes Vivantes. The restaurant is known for its hand-pulled noodles and flavorful dishes, offering a delicious alternative to traditional French fare.

Summary

The 20th Arrondissement (Ménilmontant) is a district known for its eclectic charm, rich history, and cultural diversity. From the historic Père Lachaise Cemetery and the vibrant streets of Belleville to the dynamic street art and diverse culinary scene, there's something for everyone in this lively part of Paris. Whether you're exploring the historic sites, enjoying the local arts and music scene, or sampling the diverse cuisine, the 20th Arrondissement has much to offer.

BONUS 1: PRINTABLE OFFICIAL LOUVRE GUIDE

BONUS 2: PRINTABLE PARIS MAP

BONUS 3: ONE DAY IN PARIS: THE PARIS EXPLORER GUIDEBOOK

Made in United States
Orlando, FL
18 August 2024

50532894R00065